The Elements *of* Style

Workbook

TIP TOP EDUCATION
Texas

ISBN: 978-1-64281-005-9

Table of Contents

Introduction

The Elements of Style remains one of the most widely referenced English writing guides available. Originally published in 1920, nearly 100 years ago, it has withstood the test of time, having helped countless writers improve their writing in the century since its publication. Until now, this valuable resource has only been available as a pocket reference, leaving students and aspiring authors without the pen-to-paper practice essential in order to master the art of writing with style. With exercises included, this workbook version of *The Elements of Style* solves this problem.

In the original introduction to *The Elements of Style*, William Strunk wrote:

> After [a student] has learned . . . to write plain English adequate for everyday uses, let him look, for *the secrets of style*, to the study of the masters of literature.

Along with the opportunity to practice the elementary rules of usage and elementary principles of composition presented in Strunk's original text, this updated and expanded version of *The Elements of Style* provides students with a process to study the literary works of the masters of literature, enabling novice writers to uncover the *secrets of style*. Through this process, students can also develop their own unique writing styles and cultivate the skills necessary to modify their writing styles to suit the subject, the audience, and the purpose of their writing.

In the "Secrets of Style" chapter, students analyze and imitate the writing styles of:

Ralph Waldo Emerson	Patrick Henry
George MacDonald	Victor Hugo
Mark Twain	Susan Glaspell
Charles Dickens	Jane Austen
William Shakespeare	And more . . .

In creating this text, the original chapters on form, commonly misused words and expressions, and spelling have been omitted. These standards have changed a bit in the last century. In modern high schools, colleges, and universities, students are typically required to adhere to AP, APA, MLA, or other formatting styles, each of which has its own rules for the proper formatting of written work. For that reason, students are encouraged to seek guidance from their instructors on the appropriate formatting guidelines for their written assignments. In regard to commonly misused and misspelled words, the technological advancements in and the availability of smartphones, computers, and other internet-access devices give students instant access to definitions and spelling, rendering the original versions of these lessons less necessary in the modern world.

To compile this workbook edition of *The Elements of Style*, various public-domain texts were referenced. The sources selected for this workbook were specifically chosen because they reinforce the lessons in *The Elements of Style*. For a list of sources, see the reference list on page 201.

Answer Key Included

When appropriate, answers for exercises are located in Appendix E. In some instances the answers provided are examples because the answers will vary.

The Secrets of Style

Adapted from *The Writer's Book* by James Reeve

Whole volumes have been written on style, but the heart of the matter is this: There are two elements in literature, the technical and the non-technical. The technical elements are those that deal with words, sentences, paragraphs, and the theory of the art. The non-technical element in literature is what some deem the secret of style. The secret of style is the hidden presence uniquely manifested in every author's work. The author Buffon has gone so far as to define this presence as the personality of the writer—*The style is the man.* Consequently style, in its ultimate essence, is the literary expression of the author's tastes, philosophy, and outlook on life.

With Buffon's definition in mind, an unknown author presented the question:

> If the style is the person, how can one hope to equal that style if one can never come near the person?

The author then gave the following answer:

> Be true to all you know, and see, and feel; live with the masters, and catch their spirit. You will then develop your own style.

To elaborate on that answer, to live with the masters, one must read the work of the masters; however, to catch the spirit or style of their writing, one must study and seek to emulate them. To study and learn from them, students must analyze not only the technical aspects of their writing, but the non-technical as well. By studying the style of the literary masters, students learn that the addition of a word, the omission of a phrase, or the inversion of a clause can create or alter an author's style by impacting the movement, the intensity, the emphasis, and the emotions of the author's writing. To give practice in this study of style, the final section of this text uncovers the secrets of style through the study of the literary masters.

In this workbook, the style imitation process is not meant to encourage students to acquire the style of other authors; instead, it is to help students learn to analyze the writing of others and to help students gain exposure to a variety of writing styles. As students engage in this process of analyzing and imitating other styles, students will achieve greater understanding of what a "good" writing style is and will gain greater writing flexibility, leading to the growth and enhancement of their own unique writing style and the ability to shift style at will.

To give you greater understanding of the style analysis and imitation process in this text, Benjamin Franklin's method, which provides the framework for this approach, is included below.

Benjamin Franklin's Method

In his autobiography, Benjamin Franklin explains his process of studying what he perceived to be excellent writing to develop his own writing skills:

> About this time I met with an odd volume of *The Spectator*. It was the third. I had never before seen any of them. I bought it, read it over and over, and was much delighted with it. I thought the writing excellent, and wished, if possible, to imitate it.
>
> With this in view I took some of the papers, and making short hints of the sentiment in each sentence, laid them by a few days, and then without looking at the book, tried to complete the papers again, by expressing each hinted sentiment at length, and as fully as it had been expressed before, in any suitable words that should come to hand.
>
> Then I compared my Spectator with the original, discovered some of my faults and corrected them. But I found I wanted a stock of words, or a readiness in recollecting and using them, which I thought I should have acquired before that time if I had gone on making verses . . . . Therefore I took some of the tales and turned them into verse; and after a time, when I had pretty well forgotten the prose, turned them back again.
>
> By comparing my work afterwards with the original, I discovered many faults and amended them; but I sometimes had the pleasure of fancying that, in certain particulars of small import, I had been lucky enough to improve the method or the language, and this encouraged me to think I might possibly in time come to be a tolerable English writer, of which I was extremely ambitious.

Before beginning the style exercises, there are a few suggestions or guidelines that, when followed, will aid students in the successful completion of the style writing exercises. These suggestions, listed on the following page, include general as well as specific guidelines that will help students learn to communicate more effectively.

The Steps to Improve One's Style

Adapted from *Lectures on Rhetoric* by Hugh Blair

1. **Understand your subject**. Develop clear ideas of the subject on which you are to write or speak. What we conceive clearly and feel strongly, we naturally express with clarity and strength.

2. **Write frequently and with care**. Frequency of composing is indispensably necessary. But it is not every kind of composition that will improve style. By a careless and hasty habit of writing, a bad style will be acquired. In the beginning, therefore, we ought to write slowly and with much care. Facility and speed are the fruit of experience.

3. **Read and study the works of the best authors.** No exercise, perhaps, is more useful for acquiring a proper style than translating a passage from an eminent author into our own words, and then comparing what we have written with the style of the author. This type of exercise highlights our defects, teaches us to correct them, and, through the variety of expression, moves us toward more beautiful writing.

4. **Be Yourself. Be Natural**. Caution must be used against servile imitation of any author. Mindless imitation hampers genius, and generally produces stiffness of expression. They who copy an author too closely commonly copy that author's faults as well as that author's beauties.

5. **Always adapt your style to the subject and to your audience.** When we are to write or to speak, we should fix in our minds a clear idea of our audience and our purpose. Discuss your subject with appropriate word choice, and use words that your audience understands.

6. **Write with simplicity and clarity.** *Never* leave your meaning in doubt, and always seek the expression that is most vigorous. To achieve clarity, authors should use simpler words, fewer words, and fewer figures of speech.

7. **Familiarize yourself with proper grammar.**

8. **Revise once and again. And still again.**

The Elements of Style Original Introduction

This book aims to give in brief space the principal requirements of plain English style. It aims to lighten the task of instructor and student by concentrating attention (in Chapters II and III) on a few essentials, the rules of usage and principles of composition most commonly violated. In accordance with this plan it lays down three rules for the use of the comma, instead of a score or more, and one for the use of the semicolon, in the belief that these four rules provide for all the internal punctuation that is required by nineteen sentences out of twenty. Similarly, it gives in Chapter III only those principles of the paragraph and the sentence which are of the widest application. The book thus covers only a small portion of the field of English style. The experience of its writer has been that once past the essentials, students profit most by individual instruction based on the problems of their own work, and that each instructor has his or her own body of theory, which may be preferred to that offered by any textbook.

The numbers of the sections may be used as references in correcting manuscript.

The writer's colleagues in the Department of English in Cornell University have greatly helped him in the preparation of his manuscript. Mr. George McLane Wood has kindly consented to the inclusion under Rule 10 of some material from his *Suggestions to Authors*.

The following books are recommended for reference or further study: in connection with Chapters II and IV, F. Howard Collins, *Author and Printer* (Henry Frowde); Chicago University Press, *Manual of Style*; T. L. De Vinne, *Correct Composition* (The Century Company); Horace Hart, *Rules for Compositors and Printers* (Oxford University Press); George McLane Wood, *Extracts from the Style-Book of the Government Printing Office* (United States Geological Survey); in connection with Chapters III and V, *The King's English* (Oxford University Press); Sir Arthur Quiller-Couch, *The Art of Writing* (Putnam), especially the chapter, Interlude on Jargon; George McLane Wood, *Suggestions to Authors* (United States Geological Survey); John Lesslie Hall, *English Usage* (Scott, Foresman and Co.); James P. Kelley, *Workmanship in Words* (Little, Brown and Co.). In these will be found full discussions of many points here briefly treated and an abundant store of illustrations to supplement those given in this book.

It is an old observation that the best writers sometimes disregard the rules of rhetoric. When they do so, however, the reader will usually find in the sentence some compensating merit, attained at the cost of the violation. Unless he is certain of doing as well, he will probably do best to follow the rules. After he has learned, by their guidance, to write plain English adequate for everyday uses, **let him look, for the secrets of style, to the study of the masters of literature**.

I. Elementary Rules of Usage

1. Form the possessive singular of nouns by adding 's.

A possessive noun modifies another noun, expressed or understood. Follow this rule whatever the final consonant. Thus write,

Charles's friend

Burns's poems

the witch's malice

Percy's store

I love to shop at Percy's.

Exceptions are the possessive of ancient proper names ending in *-es* and *-is*, the possessive *Jesus'*, and such forms as *for conscience' sake, for righteousness' sake*. But such forms as *Achilles' heel, Moses' laws, Isis' temple* are commonly replaced by

the heel of Achilles

the laws of Moses

the temple of Isis

The possessive plural is formed by

1) adding the apostrophe and *-s* if the noun does not end in *-s*,

the children's books

the oxen's yokes

2) adding the apostrophe alone if the noun does end in *s*.

the girls' league

the boys' club

The pronominal possessives (possessive pronouns) *hers, its, theirs, yours,* and *ours* have no apostrophe.

Note: It is common for many to confuse the following pronouns, possessives, and contractions.

it	its	it's	(it is)
your	yours	you're	(you are)
who	whose	who's	(who is)

Its is the possessive form of *it*.

Yours is the possessive form of *your*.

Whose is the possessive form of *who*.

➢ **EXERCISE 1.1: Possessives**
Write sentences using the possessive of each of the following.

1. boys

_____

_____

2. children

_____

_____

3. Charles

_____

_____

4. team

_____

_____

5. hair

_____

_____

6. *its*, the contraction *it's* in one sentence

_____

_____

7. *yours*, the contraction *you're*, and *your* in one or two sentences

_____

_____

_____

8. *whose*, the contraction *who's*, and *who* in one or two sentences

_____

_____

_____

2. In a series of three or more terms with a single conjunction, use a comma after each term except the last.

Thus write,

>   red, white, and blue
>   gold, silver, or copper
>   He opened the letter, read it, and made a note of its contents.

>   This final comma before the conjunction, called the serial comma, adds clarity.

>   For breakfast, he had eggs, toast, and orange juice.

>   confusing   He ate cake, cookies, raisins and chocolate chip muffins.
>   clear   He ate cake, cookies, raisins, and chocolate chip muffins.

In the names of business firms the last comma is omitted, as,

>   Brown, Shipley & Co.

➢ **EXERCISE 2.1: Serial commas**
   Write five sentences with serial commas.

1. _____

_____

2. _____

_____

3. _____

_____

4. _____

_____

5. _____

_____

3. Enclose parenthetic expressions between commas.

The best way to see a country, unless you are pressed for time, is to travel on foot.

This rule is difficult to apply; it is frequently hard to decide whether a single word, such as *however*, or a brief phrase is or is not parenthetic. If the interruption to the flow of the sentence is but slight, the writer may safely omit the commas. But whether the interruption be slight or considerable, never insert one comma and omit the other. Such punctuation as written below is indefensible.

incorrect	Marjorie's husband, Colonel Nelson paid us a visit yesterday.
incorrect	My brother you will be pleased to hear, is now in perfect health.

Always to be regarded as parenthetic and to be enclosed between commas are the following:

the year, when forming part of a date;
February to July, 2016
April 6, 2017

the day of the month, when following the day of the week;
Monday, November 11, 1998

the abbreviations *etc.* and *Jr.*
Lessons 21, 22, etc., are to be omitted.

Nonrestrictive relative clauses are those clauses that do not serve to identify the preceding noun. These clauses are enclosed between commas.

The audience, which had at first been indifferent, became more and more interested.

In this sentence the clause introduced by *which* does not identify which of any number of possible audiences is meant. The sentence is virtually a combination of two statements that might have been made independently.

The audience had at first been indifferent.
The audience became more and more interested.

Restrictive clauses, clauses that restrict or limit, are not set off by commas. They are needed to make the meaning of the sentence clear.

The candidate who best meets these requirements will be hired.

Here the clause introduced by *who* tells which type of any number of possible candidates is meant. The clause tells that only the candidate *who best meets these requirements* is the candidate who will be hired.

Similar clauses introduced by *where* and *when* are similarly punctuated.

> Nether Stowey, where Coleridge wrote *The Rime of the Ancient Mariner*, is a few miles from Bridgewater.

Nether Stowey is completely identified by its name; the statement about Coleridge is therefore supplementary and parenthetic—nonrestrictive.

> The day will come when you will admit your mistake.

The *day* is identified only by the dependent clause, which is therefore restrictive.

> ➢ **EXERCISE 3.1: Commas**
> Place commas where they belong in the following sentences.

1. The old man who slowly lifted his head saw us on the bank of the stream.
2. The diamond which is pure carbon is produced by intense heat and under great pressure.
3. Jeff who my sister is dating is a rocket scientist.
4. The man who set the fire has not been found.
5. He who fights and runs away may live to fight another day.
6. The Greek philosopher Diogenes sought in vain for an honest man.
7. Peter the Hermit preached the first crusade.
8. George Washington the first president of the U. S. was first in war, first in peace, and first in the hearts of his countrymen.

Compose six sentences. Write three with a restrictive clause (no commas) and three with a nonrestrictive clause (with commas).

1. _____

_____

_____

2. _____

_____

_____

3. _____

_____

_____

4. _____

_____

_____

5. _____

_____

_____

6. _____

_____

_____

When phrases and dependent clauses precede the main clause of a sentence, they are also set off by commas.

When you send for him, he will come.

Partly by hard fighting, partly by diplomatic skill, they enlarged their dominions to the east and rose to royal rank with the possession of Sicily, exchanged afterwards for Sardinia.

Entering the house, he found it empty and forlorn.

➢ **EXERCISE 3.3: Commas**
Add commas to the following sentences.

1. If you wish to talk I will be home this evening.
2. To be completely honest I am wearied by his behavior.
3. In spite of all difficulties they resolved to make an attempt at mediation.
4. While the world lasts fashion will continue to lead it by the nose.
5. As my heart was subdued by all I heard I fell down at her feet.
6. Because we wanted to see the country we traveled slowly.
7. When spring comes the flowers bloom.

> **EXERCISE 3.4: Introductory Elements**
Compose six sentences with introductory elements. Punctuate properly.

1. _____

_____

_____

2. _____

_____

_____

3. _____

_____

_____

4. _____

_____

_____

5. _____

_____

_____

6. _____

_____

_____

4. *Place a comma before a conjunction introducing an independent clause.*

A *clause* is a collection of words with both a subject and a verb. There are two types of clauses: independent, or main, and dependent, or subordinate. An *independent clause* can stand alone. A *dependent clause* requires conjoining with an independent clause to form a complete sentence. The sentence below is composed of two independent clauses, punctuated with a comma and joined by a coordinating conjunction.

Susan loves her trips to the mountains, but she does not get to go often.

Clauses can be joined with a conjunction that shows a relationship between the ideas contained in the two clauses, such as augmentation, contrast, or cause and effect. Coordinating conjunctions always come between the two independent clauses and are preceded by a comma.

Coordinating Conjunctions (a complete list)
for   and   nor   but   or   yet   so

Subordinating conjunctions head the dependent clause and travel with that dependent clause in sentence placement with a mandatory comma following the dependent clause when the dependent clause begins the sentence. The sentences below are composed of one dependent and one independent clause, punctuated properly in both instances.

Susan loves her trips to the mountains even though it often rains while she's there.
Even though it often rains while she's there, Susan loves her trips to the mountains.

Subordinating Conjunctions (an incomplete list)

cause and effect	conditions or comparisons	when, where, or how
because	although	as
since	if	after
so	since	before
for	unless	when
	than	while
	though	where
	as	since

Sentences using coordinating conjunctions are called *compound* sentences, while sentences using subordinating conjunctions are called *complex* sentences. The sentence below is a compound sentence.

The early <u>records</u> of the city <u>have disappeared</u>, and the <u>story</u> of its first years <u>can</u> no longer <u>be reconstructed</u>.

Sentences of this type, isolated from their context, may appear as if they need to be rewritten. Because the sentence makes complete sense when the comma is reached, the second clause can have the appearance of being an afterthought. Further, *and* is the least specific of connectives. Used between independent clauses, it indicates only that a relation exists between them without defining that relation. In the example above, the actual relation is that of cause and result.

The sentence might be rewritten into a complex sentence creating greater clarity in regards to the relationship between to the two clauses.

As the early records of the city have disappeared, the story of its first years can no longer be reconstructed.

Because the early records of the city have disappeared, the story of its first years can no longer be reconstructed.

In the above example sentence, the idea that the city's early story can no longer be reconstructed is the dominant point, so placing that idea in an independent clause while subordinating the other clause helps highlight the dominance of that idea in the sentence for the reader.

Consider the following compound sentence,

The situation is perilous, but there is still one chance of escape.

This sentence assigns the ideas in both clauses equal weight. It may also be rewritten as a complex sentence and made clearer through the use of subordination.

Although the situation is perilous, there is still one chance of escape.

Or the subordinate clauses might be replaced by phrases, which always terminate with a comma when they precede the main clause:

Owing to the disappearance of the early records of the city, the story of its first years can no longer be reconstructed.

In this perilous situation, there is still one chance of escape.

➢ **EXERCISE 4.1: Conjunctions**
Combine the following pairs of sentences in two ways—first using a coordinating conjunction and second using a subordinating conjunction.

1. They are determined to have their own way.
They know they will suffer for their willfulness.

_____

_____

_____

_____

2. I cannot go to the circus.
I have no money.

_____

_____

_____

_____

3. He cannot go to the circus.
No one gave him a ticket.

_____

_____

_____

_____

4. He walks slowly.
He is very tired.

_____

_____

_____

_____

➢ EXERCISE 4.2: Conjunctions

Compose six sentences with conjunctions. Punctuate accurately.

1. _____

_____

_____

2. _____

_____

_____

3. _____

_____

_____

4. _____

_____

_____

5. _____

_____

_____

6. _____

_____

_____

5. Do not join independent clauses by a comma.

If two or more independent clauses grammatically complete and not joined by a coordinating conjunction are to form a single compound sentence, the proper mark of punctuation is a **semicolon**.

> Stevenson's romances are entertaining; they are full of exciting adventures.
> It is nearly half past five; we cannot reach the woods before dark.

It is of course equally correct to write the above as two sentences each, replacing the semicolons by periods.

> Stevenson's romances are entertaining. They are full of exciting adventures.
> It is nearly half past five. We cannot reach town before dark.

If a conjunction is inserted the proper mark is a comma. (See Rule 4.)

> Stevenson's romances are entertaining, for they are full of exciting adventures.
> It is nearly half past five, and we cannot reach town before dark.

A comparison of the three forms given above will show clearly the advantage of the first. It is, at least in the examples given, better than the second form because it suggests the close relationship between the two statements in a way that the second does not attempt. It is also better than the third because it is briefer and therefore more forcible. Indeed, this simple method of indicating relationship between statements is one of the most useful devices of composition. The relationship, as above, is commonly one of cause or of consequence.

Note that if the second clause is preceded by an adverb, such as *accordingly, besides, then, therefore,* or *thus,* and not by a conjunction, the semicolon is still required, as the adverb does not change the independent nature of the clause it fronts.

> I had never been in the place before; therefore, I had difficulty in finding my way about.

Two exceptions to the rule may be admitted. If the clauses are very short, and are alike in form, a comma is usually permissible:

> Man proposes, God disposes.
> The gate swung apart, the bridge fell, the portcullis was drawn up.
> I hardly knew him, he was so changed.

Note: Joining two independent clauses with a comma is known as a *comma splice.* Some instructors consider all comma splices to be unacceptable.

➢ **EXERCISE 5.1: Semicolons**

Compose six sentences, each with two independent clauses joined by semicolons. Be sure that the two independent clauses have a close relationship.

1. _____

_____

_____

2. _____

_____

_____

3. _____

_____

_____

4. _____

_____

_____

5. _____

_____

_____

6. _____

_____

_____

➢ **EXERCISE 5.2: Exceptions to the Use of Semicolons**

Compose two short sentences that are alike in form. Join the two independent clauses by a comma rather than a semicolon.

1. _____

_____

2. _____

_____

6. Do not break sentences in two.

In other words, do not use periods for commas. The result is a sentence fragment.

incorrect	I met them on a Cunard liner several years ago. Coming home from Liverpool to New York.
incorrect	He was an interesting talker. A man who had traveled all over the world and lived in half a dozen countries.

In both of these examples, the first period should be replaced by a comma and the following word begun with a small letter.

correct	I met them on a Cunard liner several years ago, coming home from Liverpool to New York.
correct	He was an interesting talker, a man who had traveled all over the world and lived in half a dozen countries.

Recall that clauses have both a subject and a verb, while phrases have either a subject or a verb but not both. Independent clauses form complete sentences. Dependent clauses and phrases do not form complete sentences. When a dependent clause or phrase is punctuated as a full sentence, it becomes a sentence *fragment*.

The italicized words are phrases.

Seeing her nephew in the room, Mrs. Carr reproached him bitterly.
The woman, *having finished her work,* went home.
The work *just completed* is very valuable.

Here, the italicized words form a dependent clause.

If you want to see her before she leaves, you need to hurry to the airport.

> **EXERCISE 6.1: Fragments**
  Using the fragments below, compose a sentence in which you correctly use the clause or phrase given.

1. That we had taken him by surprise

_____

_____

2. When we rose the next morning, having slept well

_____

_____

3. Through no fault of his

_____

_____

4. Though the whole experience left no pleasant memory

_____

_____

5. To relieve his suffering somewhat

_____

_____

6. If that is true and if conditions are as favorable as you say

_____

_____

7. When Earth's last picture is painted

_____

_____

It is permissible to make an emphatic word or expression serve the purpose of a sentence and to punctuate it accordingly:

> Again and again he called out. No reply.

The writer must, however, be certain that the emphasis is warranted, and that no blunder in syntax or in punctuation will be suspected.

Rules 3, 4, 5, and 6 cover the most important principles in the punctuation of ordinary sentences; they should be so thoroughly mastered that their application becomes second nature.

7. A participial phrase at the beginning of a sentence must refer to the grammatical subject.

Participles or participial phrases must be placed close to the word that they modify, and the relationship between the participle or participial phrase and the modified word must be clear. If the participle or participial phrase is not clearly modifying a word in the sentence, it is a *dangling participle*. If the participle or participial phrase is not close in proximity to the word that it modifies, it is a *misplaced participle*.

> Walking slowly down the road, he saw a woman accompanied by two children.

The word *walking* refers to the subject of the sentence (*he*), not to the woman. If the writer wishes to make it refer to the woman, the sentence must be recast:

> He saw a woman, accompanied by two children, walking slowly down the road.

Participial phrases preceded by a conjunction or by a preposition, nouns in apposition, adjectives, and adjective phrases come under the same rule if they begin the sentence.

On arriving in Chicago, his friends met him at the station.	On arriving in Chicago, he was met by his friends at the station.
A soldier of proved valor, they entrusted him with the defense of the city.	A soldier of proved valor, he was entrusted with the defense of the city.
Young and inexperienced, the task seemed easy to me.	Young and inexperienced, I thought the task easy.
Without a friend to counsel him, the temptation proved irresistible.	Without a friend to counsel him, he found the temptation irresistible.

Sentences violating this rule are often ludicrous.

> Being in a dilapidated condition, I was able to buy the house very cheap.
> Wondering irresolutely what to do next, the clock struck twelve.

➤ EXERCISE 7.1: Dangling and Misplaced Modifiers

Point out the dangling or misplaced participles in the following sentences. Correct and rewrite the sentences on the lines provided.

1. While eating my dinner yesterday evening, the telephone rang.

_____

_____

2. Writing a very tedious essay, naturally the laughter of my friends on the campus disturbed me.

_____

_____

3. Peeping through our keyhole, the cat which we had mistaken for a burglar could be plainly seen.

_____

_____

4. Failing to wind my watch, it stopped.

_____

_____

5. Dropping my watch on the hardwood floor, it was broken.

_____

_____

6. This morning John saw a large snake walking through the woods.

_____

_____

➢ **EXERCISE 7.2: Sentence Imitation**
   For each sentence below, write a sentence that imitates the structure of the given sentence.

1. On arriving in Chicago, he was met by his friends at the station.

_____

_____

_____

2. A soldier of proved valor, he was entrusted with the defense of the city.

_____

_____

3. Young and inexperienced, I thought the task easy.

_____

_____

4. Without a friend to counsel him, he found the temptation irresistible.

_____

_____

8. Write with varied sentence lengths.

In addition to varying sentence type, a writer should also vary **sentence length**. The length of your sentences, as of your paragraphs, depends partly on your habits of thought, partly on your subject, and partly on the effect you wish to produce. In regard to sentence length, it is essential to write with both long and short sentences.

What a short sentence is, or what a long sentence is, it is difficult to say precisely; however, a short sentence may consist of one, two, three, or more words. Long sentences may be composed of 20, 30, 40, or more words. Short sentences are generally comprised of a single independent clause, while long sentences tend to consist of multiple clauses and phrases.

Shorter sentences, when used in connection with longer sentences, attract attention, giving force and emphasis to thought. Short sentences following one another lose the individual prominence that comes from the contrast in sentence length and can no longer be used to give force and emphasis to thought. A succession of short sentences, nevertheless, may produce other effects quite as desirable, such as movement and intensity. As it is not an easy matter to give coherence to a multitude of short sentences, a writer is sometimes betrayed by short sentences into a choppy, jerky style that is as unpleasant to a reader as the lumbering gait of a mob of ill-ordered long sentences.

The long sentence is superior to the short sentence for the unfolding of an idea. Long sentences in succession add dignity and impressiveness to a topic and a rhythm to writing that makes them well adapted for producing the higher effects of prose.

➢ **EXERCISE 8.1: Sentence Combining**
The following is an exercise in combining simple sentences to form complex and compound sentences. Combine each set of given sentences in six different ways. The first has been done for you. Answers will vary.

1. (Example)
This man is to be pitied.
He has no friends.

1. This man has no friends, and he is to be pitied. _____
2. This man is to be pitied because he has no friends. _____
3. Because this man has no friends, he is to be pitied. _____
4. This man, who has no friends, is to be pitied. _____
5. Having no friends, the man is to be pitied. _____
6. Without friends, this man is to be pitied. _____
7. This friendless man deserves our pity. _____

2. The ostrich is unable to fly.
It has wings in disproportion to its body.

1. _____
   _____
2. _____
   _____
3. _____
   _____
4. _____
   _____
5. _____
   _____
6. _____
   _____

3. Egypt is a fertile country.
    It is annually inundated by the Nile.

1. _____

_____

2. _____

_____

3. _____

_____

4. _____

_____

5. _____

_____

6. _____

_____

4. The nerves are little threads or fibers.
    They extend from the brain.
    They spread over the whole body.

1. _____

_____

_____

2. _____

_____

_____

3. _____

_____

_____

4. _____

_____

_____

5. _____

_____

_____

6. _____

_____

_____

5.   John Gutenberg published a book.
      It was the first book known to have been printed on a printing press.
      He was aided by the patronage of John Faust.
      He published it in 1455.
      He published it in the city of Mentz.

1. _____

_____

_____

_____

2. _____

_____

_____

_____

3. _____

_____

_____

_____

4. _____

_____

_____

5. _____

_____

_____

_____

6. _____

_____

_____

_____

6. The human body is a machine.
    A watch is delicately constructed.
    This machine is more delicately constructed.
    A steam engine is complicated.
    This machine is more complicated.
    A steam engine is wonderful.
    This machine is more wonderful.

1. _____

_____

_____

_____

_____

2. _____

_____

_____

_____

_____

3. _____

_____

_____

_____

_____

_____

4. _____

_____

_____

_____

_____

_____

5. _____

_____

_____

_____

_____

_____

6. _____

_____

_____

_____

_____

_____

Break up the following long sentence into short ones, eliminating words and adding connectives as you deem necessary.

It happened one day about noon, going towards my boat, I was exceedingly surprised with the print of a man's naked foot on the shore, which was very plain to be seen in the sand: I stood like one thunderstruck, or as if I had seen an apparition; I listened, I looked round me, I could hear nothing, nor see any thing; I went up to a rising ground to look farther; I went up the shore and down the shore, but it was all one, I could see no other impression but that one, I went to it again to see if there were any more, and to observe if it might not be my fancy; but there was no room for that, for there was exactly the very print of a foot, toes, heel, and every part of a foot; how it came thither, I knew not, nor could in the least imagine.

—Daniel Defoe, *Robinson Crusoe*, 1719

➢ EXERCISE 8.3: Sentence Combining

Rewrite the following statements, combining the short sentences into longer ones. Add connectives as necessary. The finished result should be one or more paragraphs written in a much more elegant manner than the statements below.

Water is a liquid. It is composed of oxygen and hydrogen. It covers about three-fourths of the surface of the earth. It takes the form of ice. It takes the form of snow. It takes the form of vapor. The air is constantly taking up water from rivers, lakes, oceans, and damp ground. Cool air contains moisture. Heated air contains more moisture. Heated air becomes lighter. It rises. It becomes cool. The moisture is condensed into fine particles. Clouds are formed. They float across the sky. The little particles unite and form raindrops. They sprinkle the dry fields. At night the grass and flowers become cool. The air is not so cool. The warm air touches the grass and flowers. It is chilled. It loses a part of its moisture. Drops of dew are formed. Water has many uses. Men and animals drink it. Trees and plants drink it. They drink it by means of their leaves and roots. Water is a great purifier. It cleanses our bodies. It washes our clothes. It washes the dust from the leaves and the flowers. Water is a great worker. It floats vessels. It turns the wheels of mills. It is converted into steam. It is harnessed to mighty engines. It does the work of thousands of men and horses.

—Reed

_____

_____

_____

_____

_____

_____

_____

_____

_____

_____

_____

_____

9. Make the paragraph the unit of composition: one paragraph to each topic.

To put one's thoughts into words that are clear, orderly, and connected is to compose, and the result is called a *composition*. A composition may consist of a single sentence, a single paragraph, or a collection of paragraphs. A *paragraph* is a connected series of sentences that develop a single topic. From this definition, it is clear that a paragraph may be a short composition, complete in itself. Usually, however, the paragraph forms only a part of a larger composition.

The paragraph, then, is a convenient device by which the writer may bring together, for the sake of the reader, closely related ideas. Each paragraph should have but one topic, and every sentence should focus on that topic. This is called the law of unity (or oneness).

> ➤ **EXERCISE 9.1: Cohesion**
> Find and underline one or more sentences that do not properly belong to the following paragraph.

The Boyhood of Franklin

Franklin's boyhood was full of hard work. His education was very scanty, but he early showed a remarkable fondness for books. He once said that he could not remember when he did not know how to read. He was placed in school during his eighth year. This famous man is said to have invented stoves. In his tenth year he was taken from school to assist his father who was a tallow chandler and soap maker. The lad worked at this distasteful business until his twelfth year, when he was apprenticed to his brother to learn the trade of a printer. At the age of seventeen, as the result of a quarrel with his brother, he ran away from home, and finally found himself in Philadelphia with a dollar and a quarter in his pocket. One of Franklin's most celebrated writings is "Poor Richard's Almanac."

—Henry Pendexter Emerson

Paragraphs and Dialogue

In *dialogue,* each speech, even if only a single word, is a paragraph by itself. In other words, a new paragraph begins with each change of speaker. The application of this rule, when dialogue and narrative are combined, is best learned from examples in well-printed works of fiction.

When showing that the words spoken by a person or character are exactly what was said, we use direct quotations. A direct quote includes an open quote ("), the spoken words, punctuation, and an end quote ("). Typically, the first word within the quote is capitalized.

To indicate who spoke, an *attributive tag* (tag) is added. The tag may be placed at the beginning, the middle, or the end of the sentence.

Tags at the beginning of the sentence,

> Jim cried, "Yay! It's snowing!"
> Father said, "If you don't clean the garage, you cannot go to the movies."
> The exhausted babysitter begged, "Please, go to sleep."

Tags in the middle of the sentence.

> "Yay!" cried Jim. "It's snowing!"   (Two separate sentences.)
> "If you don't clean the garage," said Father, "you cannot go to the movies."
> "Please," begged the exhausted babysitter, "go to sleep."

When the tag is in the middle of the sentence, the first word of the second quote is usually **not** capitalized.

Tags at the end of the sentence:

> "Yay! It's snowing!" cried Jim.
> "If you don't clean the garage, you cannot go to the movies," said Father.
> "Please go to sleep," begged the exhausted babysitter.

If a sentence ends with a tag, place a comma, exclamation mark, or question mark **before** the end quote (") and follow up with the tag. Do not place a period between the quote and the tag.

Below is a conversation from the novel *The Adventures of Sherlock Holmes* by Sir Arthur Conan Doyle. Rewrite the paragraph and punctuate the dialogue appropriately. Remember to add paragraph breaks where necessary.

Come in! said Holmes. A man entered who could hardly have been less than six feet six inches in height, with the chest and limbs of a Hercules. His dress was rich with a richness which would, in England, be looked upon as akin to bad taste. Heavy bands of astrakhan were slashed across the sleeves and fronts of his double-breasted coat, while the deep blue cloak which was thrown over his shoulders was lined with flame-coloured silk and secured at the neck with a brooch which consisted of a single flaming beryl. Boots which extended halfway up his calves, and which were trimmed at the tops with rich brown fur, completed the impression of barbaric opulence which was suggested by his whole appearance. He carried a broad-brimmed hat in his hand, while he wore across the upper part of his face, extending down past the cheekbones, a black vizard mask, which he had apparently adjusted that very moment, for his hand was still raised to it as he entered. From the lower part of the face he appeared to be a man of strong character, with a thick, hanging lip, and a long, straight chin suggestive of resolution pushed to the length of obstinacy. You had my note? he asked with a deep harsh voice and a strongly marked German accent. I told you that I would call. He looked from one to the other of us, as if uncertain which to address. Pray take a seat said Holmes. This is my friend and colleague, Dr. Watson, who is occasionally good enough to help me in my cases. Whom have I the honour to address You may address me as the Count Von Kramm, a Bohemian nobleman. I understand that this gentleman, your friend, is a man of honour and discretion, whom I may trust with a matter of the most extreme importance. If not, I should much prefer to communicate with you alone. I rose to go, but Holmes caught me by the wrist and pushed me back into my chair. It is both, or none said he. You may say before this gentleman anything which you may say to me.

10. As a rule, begin each paragraph with a topic sentence; end it in conformity with the beginning.

Again, the object of solid paragraph construction is to aid the reader. The practice of beginning a paragraph with a topic sentence and ending with the same focus enables the reader to discover the purpose of each paragraph while reading it, and to further clarify, confirm, and retain this purpose in mind upon ending it. For this reason, the most generally useful kind of paragraph, particularly in exposition and argument, is that in which

- the topic sentence comes at or near the beginning (Sometimes the topic sentence follows a transitional sentence.);
- the supporting sentences develop the statement made in the topic sentence; and
- the final sentence either emphasizes the thought of the topic sentence or states some important consequence.

Ending with a digression, or with an unimportant detail, is particularly to be avoided. Consider,

We have no quarrel with the German people. We have no feeling toward them but one of sympathy and friendship. It was not upon their impulse that their Government acted in entering this war. It was not with their previous knowledge or approval. It was a war determined upon as wars used to be determined upon in the old, unhappy days, when peoples were nowhere consulted by their rulers and wars were provoked and waged in the interest of dynasties or of little groups of ambitious men who were accustomed to use their fellow men as pawns and tools.

—From "Wilson's War Message to Congress," President Wilson, April 2, 1917

Topic of the paragraph   German People
Idea of the paragraph   The U. S. has no quarrel with the German people.

Clearly, the first sentence is the topic sentence; the succeeding sentences explain and elaborate on the statement made in the topic sentence; and the final sentence, although a fairly long sentence, concludes with an emphasis of the thought expressed in the topic sentence.

> **EXERCISE 10.1: Topic Sentence**
  Read the following paragraph. Identify and underline the topic sentence.

The proposition is peace. Not peace through the medium of war; not peace to be hunted through the labyrinth of intricate and endless negotiations; not peace to rise out of universal discord fomented from principle in all parts of the empire; not peace to depend on the juridical determination of perplexing questions, or the precise marking the shadowy boundaries of a complex government. It is simple peace, sought in its natural course and in its ordinary haunts. It is peace sought in the principles of peace, and laid in principles purely pacific. I propose, by removing the ground of difference, and by restoring the former unsuspecting confidence of the colonies in the mother country, to give permanent satisfaction to your people; and (far from a scheme of ruling by discord,) to reconcile them to each other in the same act and by the bond of the very same interest which reconciles them to the British government.

—Edmund Burke, *Speech on Conciliation with America*

> **EXERCISE 10.2: Conclusion**
  Read the following paragraph. Identify and underline the concluding *clause*.

The tremendous sea itself, when I could find sufficient pause to look at it, in the agitation of the blinding wind, the flying stones and sand, and the awful noise, confounded me. As the high watery walls came rolling in, and, at their highest, tumbled into surf, they looked as if the least would engulf the town. As the receding wave swept back with a hoarse roar, it seemed to scoop out deep caves in the beach, as if its purpose were to undermine the earth. When some white-headed billows thundered on, and dashed themselves to pieces before they reached the land, every fragment of the late whole seemed possessed by the full might of its wrath, rushing to be gathered to the composition of another monster. Undulating hills were changed to valleys, undulating valleys (with a solitary storm-bird sometimes skimming through them) were lifted up to hills; masses of water shivered and shook the beach with a booming sound; every shape tumultuously rolled on, as soon as made, to change its shape and place, and beat another shape and place away; the ideal shore on the horizon, with its towers and buildings, rose and fell; the clouds flew fast and thick; I seemed to see a rending and upheaving of all nature.

—Charles Dickens, *David Copperfield*

> **EXERCISE 10.3: Topic Sentence**
To compose topic sentences, the writer makes an assertion about the topic. Using the topic provided, compose a topic sentence, adding an assertion as necessary. Remember that a topic sentence should be a clear and concise statement that specifies the main thought contained in a paragraph. A sample has been completed for you.

Topic: Bats
Topic Sentence: Bats use special internal radar to "see."

1. Technology in the classroom
_____

_____

2. Reduce, reuse, recycle
_____

_____

3. Farm animals
_____

_____

4. Independence Day
_____

_____

5. The president of the United States
_____

_____

Supporting Sentences

According to the writer's purpose, the supporting sentences that make up the body of the paragraph may be related to the topic sentence in one or more ways.

Supporting sentences may be incorporated to do the following:

define	give reasons or proofs
compare	state facts
contrast	state examples
describe	state causes
illustrate	state effects
quote	state consequences
narrate	

In any single paragraph, the writer may carry out one or several of these processes as deemed necessary to communicate effectively.

Note the following example.

> [1]It was chiefly in the eighteenth century that a very different conception of history grew up. [A]Historians then came to believe that their task was not so much to paint a picture as to solve a problem; to explain or illustrate the successive phases of national growth, prosperity, and adversity. [B]The history of morals, of industry, of intellect, and of art; the changes that take place in manners or beliefs; the dominant ideas that prevailed in successive periods; the rise, fall, and modification of political constitutions; in a word, all the conditions of national well-being became the subject of their works. [C]They sought rather to write a history of peoples than a history of kings. [D]They looked especially in history for the chain of causes and effects. [E]They undertook to study in the past the physiology of nations, and hoped by applying the experimental method on a large scale to deduce some lessons of real value about the conditions on which the welfare of society mainly depend.

—Lecky, *The Political Value of History*

I. Topic sentence.
   A. Explains the topic sentence; the new conception of history defined.
   B. The definition expanded with examples.
   C. The definition explained by contrast.
   D. The definition explained: another element in the new conception of history.
   E. Conclusion: an important consequence of the new conception of history.

Within the paragraph, take care to organize individual sentences carefully and thoughtfully. If the paragraph contains more than one minor point, as is often the case, be sure all information relevant to each respective point follows in logical progression. Organize this information within itself such that the

> most important precedes the less important;
> more general precedes the more specific; and
> earlier statement precedes chronologically later statements.

Include narrative devices among these ideas to both show how the ideas relate to one another and to indicate the purpose in including each idea. When moving to the second minor topic within the paragraph, be sure to give a transitional word, phrase, or clause mid-paragraph to help the reader follow your thinking. Be sure to include all necessary narrative components in the paragraph (including statements of connection between ideas and between parts of ideas where appropriate) to help the reader fully understand your purpose.

> **EXERCISE 10.4: Organization**
> On the following page, rewrite the paragraph below. Add or omit words as necessary. Be sure to:
>
> 1. Organize sentences appropriately.
> 2. Add narrative language to connect ideas.
> 3. Help the reader easily follow the flow of thought.
> 4. Add an appropriate concluding sentence.

Taro root is a starchy, nutrient-rich root vegetable. Whatever you can do with a potato, you can do with taro. It's high in fiber and has a rich antioxidant content to help fight diseases of many kinds and improve vision. Loaded with potassium, it helps with circulation. Its flavor and texture are more interesting than a potato's though. Its high vitamin C levels boost the immune system and help combat immuno-deficiency conditions. Rich also in iron and copper, taro reduces the chances of developing anemia and stimulates blood flow. It makes an easy side dish, whether mashed, simmered, stewed, or fried. It's also pretty high in calories.

If the paragraph forms part of a larger composition, its relation to the previous paragraph, or its function as a part of the whole composition, may need to be expressed. This can sometimes be done by a mere word or phrase (*again*; *therefore*; *for the same reason*) in the topic sentence. Sometimes, however, it is expedient to precede the topic sentence by one or more *transitional sentences*. A transitional sentence demonstrates the direction of thought of the writer by establishing a bridge from the previous subdivision to the next.

Examples of transitional sentences:

Really unselfish action in peace or war *does something more than* make a man himself great. It helps others to be like him.

Unfortunately, they are wrong. The world is more than a game of cards.

There is another line of prophecy, however, which is, I believe, quite as interesting and far easier. If I were forced to turn seer and to undertake to forecast future events, and could I have my choice of fields, I would keep quite clear of any attempt at forecasting future financial affairs and would adopt the easier course of attempting to predict the measure of success or failure that is likely, with added years, to come to a young man.

The first two examples given illustrate additional uses of the transitional sentence. Besides showing the transition, the first emphasizes the theme of the paragraph, and the second points out a contrasting idea. The third shows that the writer is taking up another division of the essay.

Note on paragraph division: If the subject about which you are writing is of slight extent, or if you intend to treat it very briefly, there may be no need for subdivision. Thus, a brief description, a brief summary of a literary work, a brief account of a single incident, or a brief narrative merely outlining an action may be complete in a single paragraph. After the paragraph has been written, examine it to see whether it will benefit from further division.

Ordinarily, however, a general subject requires division into topics, each of which should be made the subject of a paragraph. The objective of treating each topic in a paragraph by itself is, of course, to aid the reader. The beginning of each paragraph is a signal to the reader that a new step in the development of the subject has been reached.

The extent of subdivision will vary with the length of the composition. For example, a shorter book or poem might consist of a single topic addressed in a single paragraph. One slightly longer might consist of two topics addressed in two paragraphs:

I.   Account of the work
II.   Critical discussion

A novel might be discussed in four paragraphs with the following topics:

I.   Setting
II.   Plot
III. Characters
IV.   Theme

A historical event might be discussed in three paragraphs with the following topics:

I.   Causes of the event
II.   Account of the event
III. Consequences of the event

➢ **EXERCISE 10.5: Transitions**

For each blank line, write a transition sentence or clause that will act as a bridge from the previous paragraph to the current. (If you add a clause only, correct the punctuation of the sentence that follows the added transitional clause to create an appropriately punctuated compound or complex sentence.)

Like all other parts of your body, your teeth have to last you a lifetime. However, unlike other parts of your body, teeth don't heal themselves when they have been damaged. Once you damage a tooth, you have to have it professionally fixed. It will not heal on its own. Therefore, responsible oral care will help your teeth last long into your elder years.

_____

Brushing your teeth regularly helps ensure your teeth will last for many years. Brushing removes bacteria and other tiny matter that builds up on your teeth and causes problems such as cavities and periodontitis, or worse. It's important to brush carefully, ensuring you reach all surfaces of all teeth and scrub them as clean as you can with every brushing.

_____

Flossing your teeth every day is important. Dental floss reaches in between your teeth where your brush doesn't reach and cleans the gum area between your teeth as well as the sides of your teeth.

_____

Visiting a dentist regularly for a cleaning and examination helps ensure your teeth remain healthy. With their tiny equipment, dentists can see problem areas just beginning to form and guide you to best avoid them through targeted oral care.

11. Write with a purpose.

For every paragraph, it is necessary to understand the purpose of your composition.

The Purpose: Narration—Narration is that form of composition which deals with events or objects in action. People and things act or are acted upon. Life is a continued series of actions, and any composition—oral or written—that recounts in order the happenings of any part of it, or gives the details of any single event in it, is a narrative. A young girl returns from a mountain climbing expedition and relays the events to her friends. A college student witnesses a riot and writes about it in the university newspaper. An aspiring historian becomes intensely interested in the Wars of the Roses, or the life of Shakespeare, and collects the intricate details into a historical text. An incident fires the imagination of a novelist, and from a few meager details, he builds a thrilling drama. All of these are narratives.

The following is a simple narrative in which the events of a few minutes are narrated in the order of their occurrence. Notice the humorous tone with which this particular narrative is written.

Peter's Declamation

A friend of mine, Peter by name, had selected for his speech that extract from Patrick Henry's famous oration, which begins with the words, "I have but one lamp by which my feet are guided, and that is the lamp of experience." When his name was called, Peter confidently mounted the rostrum; but although he had quietly memorized his piece in his own room, he had not accustomed his ears to his own voice in declamation. He shouted from the stage, "I have but one lamp—lamp—lamp," and he could get no further. His speech had gone from his memory. He passed his left hand across his forehead in a vain effort to recall it; while with his right he pulled at his trousers as if he thought it might have slipped down into his pocket; but it came not. He began again, "I have but one lamp—lamp—lamp;" and then the teacher, to the amusement of the school, said, "Come down, Peter; your lamp has gone out."

–Henry Pendexter Emerson

To write a narrative, the chronological events of an incident are relayed. Each occurrence of the incident must be expanded upon by the addition of details that show, moment by moment, what has occurred.

An outline of the narrative writing process looks like the following:

I. *The Incident or Topic. Event to be narrated*
   A. *Topic Sentence (The Summary):* A summary of the incident, listing primary details.
   B. *The Expansion:* List the facts of the incident in chronological order.
   C. *The Enlargements:* To make the composition complete, we must introduce new facts that will explain the connections between events. Also include description as needed.

I. *Topic: Peter's Declamation*

   A. *Topic Sentence:* Peter practiced for his speech, but when it came time for him to recite it, he became confused by the echo of his own voice and forgot everything.
   B. *The Expansion*:
      1. Peter selected a speech.
      2. "I have but one lamp by which my feet are guided, and that is the lamp of experience."
      3. Peter was called, mounted the rostrum.
      4. He had practiced and memorized his speech.
      5. Peter shouted, and his voice echoed.
      6. He stopped.
      7. He forgot everything.
      8. He pressed his hand to his forehead.
      9. He pulled at his trousers.
      10. He started again, "I have but one lamp—lamp—lamp . . ."
      11. Teacher said, "Come down. Your lamp has gone out."
   C. *The Enlargements:* Add descriptive adjectives, dialogue, and appropriate adverbs.

The finished narrative is a combination of the expansion and the enlargements subtopics.

➢ **EXERCISE 11.1: Outlining a Narrative**
In the template below, create an outline for a narrative composed of a single paragraph. Choose a scene from a favorite novel. Relay the events in chronological order, using transitions as appropriate.

I. Topic: _____

  A. *Topic Sentence:* _____

    _____

    _____

  B. *The Expansion*: *Chronological Order*

    1. _____

    2. _____

    3. _____

    4. _____

    5. _____

    6. _____

    7. _____

    8. _____

    9. _____

    10. _____

  C. *The Enlargements:* Add descriptive adjectives, dialogue, and appropriate adverbs. Avoid weak verbs and adjectives such as nice, bad, pretty, etc.

On the following page, write the finished narrative, which is a combination of the expansion and the enlargements.

➢ **EXERCISE 11.2: Writing a Narrative Paragraph**
On the lines that follow, write a narrative paragraph for the outline created in the previous exercise.

_____

_____

_____

_____

_____

_____

_____

_____

_____

_____

_____

_____

_____

_____

_____

_____

_____

_____

_____

_____

_____

_____

_____

_____

_____

> ➤ **EXERCISE 11.3: Outlining a Narrative**
> In the template below, create an outline for a narrative composed of a single paragraph. Tell of an actual event from your past. Relay the events in chronological order, using transitions as appropriate.

I. Topic: _____

  A. *Topic Sentence:* _____

     _____

     _____

  B. *The Expansion*: *Chronological Order*

    1. _____

    2. _____

    3. _____

    4. _____

    5. _____

    6. _____

    7. _____

    8. _____

    9. _____

    10. _____

  C. *The Enlargements:* Add descriptive adjectives, dialogue, and appropriate adverbs. Avoid weak verbs and adjectives such as nice, bad, pretty, etc.

The finished narrative is a combination of the expansion and the enlargements.

➢ EXERCISE 11.4: Writing a Narrative Paragraph

On the lines that follow, write a narrative paragraph for the outline created in the previous exercise.

_____

_____

_____

_____

_____

_____

_____

_____

_____

_____

_____

_____

_____

_____

_____

_____

_____

_____

_____

_____

_____

_____

_____

_____

_____

The Purpose: Description—The writer's general aim or purpose in description is to paint a picture through words in such a way that others may see the picture as the writer sees it. If the writer were to describe a particular sunset scene that had appealed to her strongly, her purpose might be to portray the whole changing process from the declining sun to the increasing dusk, or it might be to portray the scene as it was at one particular moment. Either way, the writer's purpose is to create an image and atmosphere through words that allow the reader to envision the subject in the manner desired by the writer.

When writing a descriptive paragraph, word choice, effective modifier use, and good sentence structure are critical. The effect of words in combination, when written well, emphasize the atmosphere or mood the writer wishes to create.

Consider the following:

> As he addressed another part of the audience, his back was turned toward us. He was tall and straight. His shoulders were broad and square. His head was massive and was covered with iron-gray hair. All became silent as he turned around.

> He has a round face and deep-set, dark-brown eyes. His forehead is broad and firmly outlined. He has a fair complexion with rosy cheeks, which indicate good health. His nose is short and thick. His ears are well proportioned to his face and lie close to his head. His athletic body is well developed.

In both paragraphs above, the short, simple sentences all built on the same plan are appropriate only to students in lower grades. Such writing is entirely without art and does little more than furnish a list of items. To truly describe, the writer must choose words and structure sentences so that the result is prose that describes and creates the appropriate tone and mood.

Consider the descriptive paragraph below. Notice the strength of the nouns, verbs, and adjectives used.

> Oh! But he was a tight-fisted hand at the grindstone, Scrooge! A squeezing, wrenching, grasping, scraping, clutching, covetous old sinner! Hard and sharp as flint, from which no steel had ever struck out generous fire; secret, and self-contained, and solitary as an oyster. The cold within him froze his old features, nipped his pointed nose, shriveled his cheek, stiffened his gait; made his eyes red, his thin lips blue; and spoke out very shrewdly in his grating voice. A frosty rim was on his head, and on his eyebrows, and his wiry chin. He carried his own low temperature always about with him; he iced his office in dog-days; and didn't thaw it one degree at Christmas.

> —Charles Dickens, *A Christmas Carol*

The general outline of a descriptive paragraph will often contain the following:

I. Topic
   A. *Topic Sentence:*
      1. Clear definition. Class to which the object belongs.
      2. Points of agreement and difference between it and other objects of the same class.
   B. *Details and Illustrations:*
      1. Appearance, form, size, color.
      2. Locality or situation.
      3. Structure, with a description of its parts.
      4. Characteristic features or points of special interest.
      5. Habits and behaviors.
   C. *Reflections:* its qualities, its uses, closure.

Note: Which details and illustrations to include are determined by the topic you are describing. If describing something that is nontangible, you would not include appearance but some other manner by which you can differentiate it from like items in the same class or category.

A possible outline for the Scrooge description is as follows:

I. Topic: Scrooge
   A. *Topic Sentence:*
      1. Tight-fisted (stingy)
      2. Covetous old sinner (group or class to which he belonged)
   A. *Details and Illustrations:*
      1. Flint with illustration
      2. Secret with illustration
      3. Cold from inside
      4. Describe nose, cheeks, gait, eyes, lips, voice, head, eyebrows, chin
      5. Carried cold with him
   B. *Reflections:* iced his office in summer, didn't thaw at Christmas

> **EXERCISE 11.5: Outlining a Descriptive Paragraph**
> Using the outline templates on this page and the next, outline two different descriptive paragraphs. Possible topics include:

sunset or landscape	interesting person or character
sweet pet or vicious beast	natural wonder of the world
vacation destination	aftermath of a natural disaster

I. Topic: _____

  A. *Topic Sentence:*

    1. Class to which the object belongs: _____

    _____

    2. Difference between it and other objects of the same class:_____

    _____

  B. *Details and Illustrations:*

    1. _____

    _____

    2. _____

    _____

    3. _____

    _____

    4. _____

    _____

    5. _____

    _____

    6. _____

    _____

    7. _____

    _____

  C. *Reflections: its qualities, its uses, closure.*_____

    _____

II. Topic: _____

    A. *Topic Sentence:*

       1. Class to which the object belongs: _____

          _____

          _____

       2. Difference between it and other objects of the same class: _____

          _____

          _____

    B. *Details and Illustrations:*

       1. _____

          _____

       2. _____

          _____

       3. _____

          _____

       4. _____

          _____

       5. _____

          _____

       6. _____

          _____

       7. _____

          _____

    C. *Reflections: its qualities, its uses, closure*_____

          _____

➤ **EXERCISE 11.6: Descriptive Paragraphs**
On the lines that follow, write a descriptive paragraph for the Topic I outline from the previous exercise. On the following page, write a descriptive paragraph for the Topic II outline.

Topic I Paragraph:

_____

_____

_____

_____

_____

_____

_____

_____

_____

_____

_____

_____

_____

_____

_____

_____

_____

_____

_____

_____

_____

Topic II Paragraph:

The Purpose: Exposition—The purpose of the exposition (expository) paragraph is to explain. The usual form of the paragraph, therefore, is the statement of a fact as true, followed by an explanation of the way in which it is true, so that the reader will understand it as the writer understands it. Expository paragraphs may be developed in various ways.

The expository paragraph may be developed by any combination of the following supporting details:

Analogy	Definition
Analysis	Description
Causes	Details
Classification	Effects
Comparison	Events
Consequences	Examples
Contrast	Narrative
Paraphrasing	Process Analysis

The expository paragraph may also be developed through the use of only one of the supporting details above. When only one detail is used, it must be fully developed, and the paragraph must still provide explanation that will enable the reader to understand the topic.

Consider the three expository paragraphs below. In the first, a statement is made, the truth of which is made clear by definition, details, and process. In the second, an effect is stated and the causes are given by way of narrative and explanation. In the third, a paraphrase is written and expanded by way of illustrations and examples.

Definition, Details, and Process

Fishing with a garden rake and a bicycle lamp is not sport, but it has been found profitable in England, where fish are raised for the market in much the same manner as pigs or chickens. The fish-cultivator utilizes stiff clay lands, which are not valuable for agricultural purposes, and digs a number of rather shallow ponds supplied with water from a convenient stream. These ponds are stocked with such coarse fish as find a ready market—roach, perch, bream, and eels. The harvesting of the fish is most easily accomplished at night, the fishing paraphernalia consisting of an ordinary garden rake, a good bicycle lamp, or electric bull's eye, and a basket. When the bright light is thrown upon the water, the fish crowd into the lighted area in such numbers that the larger ones—the only ones that should be taken from the ponds, of course—may be readily raked ashore and placed in the basket.

—Carolyn M. Gerrish

Pope in the end became an avowed enemy to Addison. There were several *causes* that led to this result. The first of these was the John Dennis affair. Dennis had made an attack upon Addison, and Pope replied without the knowledge of the latter. Addison disapproved of Pope's course and told him so. Then came the misunderstanding over the rewriting of *The Rape of the Lock.* Pope asked Addison's advice, and he gave it. Pope decided to follow a contrary course, and succeeded. He then imagined that the advice had been given through malice. But it was the rival translations of the *Iliad* that caused the total rupture of friendly relations between the two men. Pope asked Addison to read his translation of the first book of the *Iliad.* Addison replied that he would have been glad to do so, but that he had already promised to perform a similar office for Tickell. The two translations appeared, and both were praised by Addison and his followers. Pope, however, imagined that a conspiracy had been formed against him, and that Addison was at the bottom of it. The already strained relations were entirely and permanently broken.

—Stebbins

Paraphrase can be expanded with comments, illustrations and reflections. A paraphrase requires that the writer express a thought in *different words* and a *different structure.*

"Tis better to have loved and lost,
Than never to have loved at all."

—Tennyson

When we lose a very dear friend, we are apt to think that we might have been spared the trial and suffering of bereavement had we never known him, and even to wish that it had been so. A little reflection, however, will convince us that we have gained inestimable advantages both by the friendship itself and by its loss. That man is not to be envied who has never had a friend to lose. The best feelings of his nature lie dormant, and his affections, having no external object to which to cling, hang loose and useless, or entwine themselves around his own heart and choke its growth. Nothing is more despicable than to see a man wrapped up continually in his own heart, living for himself alone, seeking only what ministers to his own pleasure, or gratifies his own vanity. There is a joy, on the other hand, in the mere outflowing of affection, in the enkindling of generous sentiments, in the performance of little acts of kindness, which strengthens our nature, and makes us in every sense better men. Even the bereaved mother, in her deepest grief, has sources of joy which the childless cannot understand.

—Walter Scott Dalgleish

Paraphrasing also requires that the writer grasp the thought, make it her own, and then express it in original language. For example, one may clarify an abstract truth by expressing it in a concrete form, or *vice versa*. The general truth that men's ill deeds are remembered after their good deeds are forgotten is expressed by Shakespeare in contrasted metaphors when he says,

> "Men's evil manners live in brass;
> Their virtues we write in water."

And he repeats the same truth under a different image in the lines,

> "The evil that men do lives after them;
> The good is oft interred with their bones."

In these examples, Shakespeare paraphrased himself. As writers, we often draw from the ideas and words of others, and these expressions require either exact repetition within quotation marks or paraphrasing with no quotation marks. Please note that changing merely a couple of words in a sentence is not enough to create a viable paraphrase—the entire way of expressing the idea must be changed for true paraphrasing to occur.

Note: Whether quoting or paraphrasing another author's work, attribution must be given in order to avoid plagiarism. To properly document your sources, follow the method outlined by your instructor.

➤ **EXERCISE 11.7. Paraphrasing**
Paraphrase the following. Use a thesaurus as necessary. (Answers will vary.)

1. In order to retain mobility as we age, we must incorporate adequate exercise into our daily routine from a fairly young age. _____

   _____

   _____

   _____

2. Happiness is a matter of personal choice: If you choose to live in a happy disposition, you can and you will. _____

   _____

   _____

   _____

3. Humans are made to dream, and dreams are made to be followed. _____

   _____

   _____

4. One of the most fascinating aspects of our complex ecosystem is how the same plant requires different tending in different climates. _____

   _____

   _____

5. Furthering your skills in writing will pay off in countless ways and for the rest of your life. _____

   _____

   _____

As you can see, expository paragraphs come in many forms, developed via many methods; however, when writing an expository paragraph, take caution. It is not sufficient to simply list details and then write them in the shape of a paragraph. In a well-written expository paragraph, whenever it is helpful to the reader, supplementary information will include a statement or clause that further explains or illustrates the subtopic information, creating a well-written paragraph that flows from clause to clause. Consider the italicized phrases or clauses that were added to the subtopic information in the fishing paragraph.

The fish-cultivator utilizes stiff clay lands.	The fish-cultivator utilizes stiff clay lands, *which are not valuable for agricultural purposes.* (tells which and why)
The fish-cultivator digs a number of rather shallow ponds.	The fish-cultivator digs a number of rather shallow ponds *supplied with water from a convenient stream.* (tells which)
The fish crowd into the lighted area.	*When the bright light is thrown upon the water,* the fish crowd into the lighted area. (tells how)

To add more information to your subtopics, consider adding clauses that inform by telling who, when, where, why, which, or how.

The general outline for the exposition paragraph contains the topic sentence, the combination of any subtopic details, supplementary information (adding who, when, where, why, which, or how) and the conclusion. A general outline is on the following page.

I. Topic
  A. *Topic Sentence*
    1. Background information
    2. Background information
  B. *Exposition: Development via any method necessary for adequate explanation*
    1. Definition of terms, if necessary (what is or is not)
    2. Analogy
    3. Analysis
    4. Causes
    5. Classification
    6. Comparison
    7. Consequences
    8. Contrast
    9. Definition
    10. Description
    11. Details
    12. Effects
    13. Events
    14. Examples
    15. Narrative
    16. Process Analysis
  C. *Conclusion: Summary or Amplification*
    1. Advantages and disadvantages
    2. Approval or disapproval
    3. Feelings of pleasure or pain

An outline of the "fishing with a rake" paragraph looks like the following:

I. Topic: Fishing with a garden rake
  A. *Topic Sentence*
    1. Background information: profitable in England
    2. Background information (comparison): fish raised for market, like farm animals
  B. *Exposition: Explanation via Necessary Methods*
    1. Definition: not sport
    2. Details: stiff clay lands
    3. Details: creation of shallow ponds
    4. Details: type of fish
    5. Details: fishing paraphernalia
    6. Process: method of harvesting
  C. *Conclusion: Summary or Amplification*
    1. Effect: fish crowd toward the light
    2. Effect: larger ones are easily retrieved

➢ **EXERCISE 11.8: Outlining an Exposition Paragraph**
In the template below, create an outline for an expository paragraph. You may pick a topic from the list below or create your own.

Explain the benefits of budgeting   Fear is the mark of a mean spirit.
How to be a best friend   How to be successful
No pain, no gain   Finding the perfect job

I. Topic: _____

  A. *Topic Sentence*

    1. _____

      _____

    2. _____

      _____

  B. *Exposition: Development via Necessary Methods*

    1. _____

      _____

    2. _____

      _____

    3. _____

      _____

    4. _____

      _____

    5. _____

      _____

    6. _____

      _____

  C. *Reflection: Summary or Amplification*

    1. _____

      _____

    2. _____

      _____

> **EXERCISE 11.9: Writing an Expository Paragraph**
> On the lines that follow, write an exposition paragraph for the outline created in the previous exercise.

Note: When writing the expository paragraph, remember to include additional information via phrases or clauses for the supporting details in point B. Also remember that each item in your outline does not correspond to a separate sentence; instead, each item is representative of an idea that you will develop via dependent and/or independent clauses.

> **EXERCISE 11.10: Outlining an Expository Paragraph**
> Create another outline for an expository paragraph of your own. Choose a different topic from the list below, or you may make up your own topic.

Explain the benefits of budgeting

How to be a best friend

No pain, no gain

Fear is the mark of a mean spirit.

How to be successful

Finding the perfect job

I. Topic: _____

   A. *Topic Sentence*

      1. _____

         _____

      2. _____

         _____

   B. *Exposition: Development via Necessary Methods*

      1. _____

         _____

      2. _____

         _____

      3. _____

         _____

      4. _____

         _____

      5. _____

         _____

      6. _____

         _____

   C. *Reflection: Summary or Amplification*

      1. _____

         _____

      2. _____

         _____

➢ **EXERCISE 11.11: Writing an Expository Paragraph**
On the lines that follow, write an expository paragraph for the outline created in the previous exercise.

Note: When writing the expository paragraph, remember to include supporting phrases or clauses for your supporting details in point B. Also remember that each item in your outline does not correspond to a separate sentence; instead, each item is representative of an idea which you will develop via dependent and or independent clauses.

The Purpose: Persuasion. The persuasive paragraph is very similar to the narrative paragraph, the descriptive paragraph, and the exposition paragraph. The difference between persuasion and the other paragraph forms is chiefly one of purpose, which usually leads to a slight difference in wording. In the expository paragraph, the writer's primary purpose is to explain a thing as he understands it; in the narrative paragraph, the writer's primary purpose is to retell an event; and in the descriptive paragraph, the writer's primary purpose is to describe. In the persuasive paragraph, the writer's primary purpose is to convince someone via reasons and proofs that a particular view of a topic is correct.

There are several kinds of arguments that may be used in a persuasive paragraph. We may argue that a certain event has taken place or is likely to take place, because there are sufficient causes to produce the result.[I] We may also reason that something has happened, because we see the results.[II] In certain cases, things usually happen together. When we see one, we see the other. Thunder accompanies a rainstorm, but is neither a cause nor a result of it.[III] Lastly, we often argue from examples or instances. If a thing is so in one or more cases, we conclude that it will be so in a certain other similar case.[IV]

To summarize, we use the
> I. Presence of causes to prove the existence of an effect.
> II. Presence of effects to prove the existence of a cause.
> III. Presence of events to prove the existence of an accompanying circumstance.
> IV. Presence of examples or instances to prove examples or instances are possible.

Consider the following persuasive paragraph,

Although there are discoveries which are said to have been made by accident, if carefully inquired into, it will be found that there has really been very little that was accidental about them. For the most part, these so-called accidents have only been opportunities, carefully improved by genius. The fall of the apple at Newton's feet has often been quoted in proof of the accidental character of some discoveries. But Newton's whole mind had already been devoted for years to the laborious and patient investigation of the subject of gravitation; and the circumstance of the apple falling before his eyes was suddenly apprehended only as genius could apprehend it, and served to flash upon him the brilliant discovery then opening to his sight. In like manner, the brilliantly colored soap-bubbles blown from a common tobacco pipe—though "trifles light as air" in most eyes—suggested to Dr. Young his beautiful theory of "interferences," and led to his discovery relating to the diffraction of light. Although great men are popularly supposed only to deal with great things, such men as Newton and Young were ready to detect the significance of the most familiar and simple facts; their greatness consisting mainly in their wise interpretation of them.

—S. Smiles

The general outline of a persuasive paragraph will often contain some variation of the template below. It is important to remember, however, that the subtopic information under each main topic may be omitted or rearranged as necessary. It is even possible to compose an entire paragraph based on the development of one subtopic—the illustration of one cause to prove an effect.

I. Topic
   A. *Topic Sentence*
      a. Background
      b. Proposition
      c. Definition of terms
   B. *Proofs*
      a. Causes to prove the existence of an effect
      b. Effects to prove existence of a cause
      c. Events to prove the existence of an accompany circumstance
      d. Examples or illustrations to prove a particular case
   C. *Conclusion: Summary or Amplification*
      a. Advantages and disadvantages
      b. Approval or disapproval
      c. Feelings of pleasure or pain

An outline of the persuasive paragraph looks like the following:

I. Topic: Great discoveries are not by accident.
   A. *Topic Sentence*
      a. Background: Claim discoveries by accident
      b. Proposition: Upon investigation, discoveries not by accident
      c. Definition of terms: not accidents, opportunities plus genius
   B. *Proofs*
      a. Examples: Narrative of Newton and the apple
      b. Presence of Cause: Newton studied gravitation for years
      c. Presence of Effect: Newton's grasp of the simple was evidence of genius
      d. Example: Dr. Young and bubbles from pipe
      e. Presence of Effect: Young's discovery of "theory of interferences"
   C. *Conclusion: Summary or Amplification*
      a. Summary: Original claim: "great men . . . deal with great things"
      b. Summary: Presence of their ability to understand the simple, proves greatness of Newton and Young

➤ **EXERCISE 11.12: Outlining a Persuasive Paragraph**
In the template below, create an outline for a persuasive paragraph of your own. Below is a list of suggested topics:

_____should be regulated.

College should be mandatory.

_____ is the best form of government.

_____ should be illegal.

I. Topic: _____

  A. *Topic Sentence*

    1. _____

      _____

    2. _____

      _____

  B. *Proofs: Causes, effects, examples, evidence*

    1. _____

      _____

    2. _____

      _____

    3. _____

      _____

    4. _____

      _____

    5. _____

      _____

    6. _____

      _____

  C. *Conclusion: Summary or Amplification*

    1. _____

      _____

    2. _____

      _____

On the lines that follow, write a persuasive paragraph for the outline created in the previous exercise.

Like the expository paragraph, remember to include supporting phrases or clauses for the details in point B of your persuasive paragraph. Also remember that each point in your outline does not correspond to a separate sentence; rather, each point is representative of an idea that you will develop via dependent and/or independent clauses.

_____

_____

_____

_____

_____

_____

_____

_____

_____

_____

_____

_____

_____

_____

_____

_____

_____

_____

_____

_____

_____

_____

> **EXERCISE 11.14: Outlining a Persuasive Paragraph**
> In the template below, create an outline for a persuasive paragraph of your own. Below is a list of suggested topics:

College should be free.

The minimum wage should be _____.

Every person should (not) have access to free health care.

The wall of separation between church and state should (not) be abolished.

I. Topic: _____

  A. *Topic Sentence*

    1. _____

    _____

    2. _____

    _____

  B. *Proofs: Causes, effects, examples, evidence*

    1. _____

    _____

    2. _____

    _____

    3. _____

    _____

    4. _____

    _____

    5. _____

    _____

    6. _____

    _____

  C. *Conclusion: Summary or Amplification*

    1. _____

    _____

    2. _____

    _____

> **EXERCISE 11.15: Writing a Persuasive Paragraph**
> On the lines that follow, write a persuasive paragraph for the outline created in the previous exercise. For each proof you include, write at least two sentences—one to state the proof and the other to illustrate or explain the proof.

12. Use the active voice.

Verbs can be *active* or *passive*. A sentence is written in *active voice* when the subject of the sentence is performing the action of the sentence. A sentence is written in *passive voice* when the action is being done *to* the subject of the sentence. Essentially, the object of the sentence has become the subject of the sentence.

Active	Mary threw the ball to John.
	Mary is the subject; she is the one throwing the ball.
Passive	The ball was thrown to John by Mary.
	The ball is the subject; the ball is being thrown.

The active voice is usually more direct and vigorous than the passive:

> I shall always remember my first visit to Boston.

This is much better than the passive voice:

> My first visit to Boston will always be remembered by me.

The latter sentence is less direct, less bold, and less concise. If the writer tries to make it more concise by omitting "by me" —

> My first visit to Boston will always be remembered—

it becomes indefinite: Is it the writer, or some person undisclosed, or the world at large that will always remember this visit?

This rule does not, of course, mean that the writer should entirely discard the passive voice, which is frequently convenient and sometimes necessary.

> The dramatists of the Restoration are little esteemed today.
> Modern readers have little esteem for the dramatists of the Restoration.

The first would be the right form in a paragraph on the dramatists of the Restoration—the second, in a paragraph on the tastes of modern readers. The need of making a particular word the subject of the sentence will often, as in these examples, determine which voice is to be used.

As a rule, avoid making one passive depend directly upon another.

Gold was not allowed to be exported.	It was forbidden to export gold. (The export of gold was prohibited.)

In the example above, before correction, the word properly related to the second passive is made the subject of the first.

A common fault is to use a noun that expresses the entire action as the subject of a passive construction, leaving to the verb no function beyond that of completing the sentence.

A survey of this region was made in 1900.	This region was surveyed in 1900.
Mobilization of the army was rapidly effected.	The army was rapidly mobilized.
Confirmation of these reports cannot be obtained.	These reports cannot be confirmed.

Consider the sentence, "The export of gold was prohibited," in which the predicate "was prohibited" expresses something not implied in "export."

The habitual use of the active voice makes for forcible writing. This is true not only in narrative principally concerned with action but in writing of any kind. Many a tame sentence of description or exposition can be made lively and emphatic by substituting a verb in the active voice for some such perfunctory expression as *there is* or *could be heard*.

There were a great number of dead leaves lying on the ground.	Dead leaves covered the ground.
The sound of a guitar somewhere in the house could be heard.	Somewhere in the house a guitar hummed sleepily.
The reason that she left college was that her health became impaired.	Failing health compelled her to leave college.
It was not long before he was very sorry that he had said what he had.	He soon repented his words.

> **EXERCISE 12.1: Passive to Active**
> Change each of the following sentences from passive to active as appropriate.

1. The shot was heard round the world. _____

   _____

2. The boy was viciously attacked by the mountain lion._____

   _____

3. It is dreamed by many people that they would one day live in an exotic paradise and

   sip the water out of fresh coconuts every morning. _____

   _____

   _____

   _____

4. She was seen as intelligent and humorous, if mainly for her delightful command of

   satire and irony, when mixed in the proper company. _____

   _____

   _____

   _____

5. They were given a second chance, but will not be presented with the opportunity by

   this same company a third time. _____

   _____

   _____

   _____

6. Sal and Serena were wished well by their large group of smiling friends, who had

   arrived to see them off on their journey. _____

   _____

   _____

   _____

On the lines provided, imitate the sentences below by composing five pairs of sentences—one active and one passive.

Just kings **ruled** the nation.	The nation **was ruled** by just kings.
William **conquered** Harold.	Harold **was conquered** by William.
Hail **pummeled** the car.	The car **was pummeled** by hail.

1. _____

_____

2. _____

_____

3. _____

_____

4. _____

_____

5. _____

_____

13. Put statements in positive form.

Make definite assertions. Avoid tame, colorless, hesitating, non-committal language. Use the word *not* as a means of denial or in antithesis, never as a means of evasion.

He was not very often on time.	He usually came late.
He did not think that studying Latin was much use.	He thought the study of Latin useless.
The Taming of the Shrew is rather weak in spots. Shakespeare does not portray Katharine as a very admirable character, nor does Bianca remain long in memory as an important character in Shakespeare's works.	The women in *The Taming of the Shrew* are unattractive. Katharine is disagreeable, Bianca insignificant.

The last example, before correction, is indefinite as well as negative. The corrected version, consequently, is simply a guess at the writer's intention.

All three examples show the weakness inherent in the word *not*. Consciously or unconsciously, the reader is dissatisfied with being told only what is not, wishing instead to be told what is. Hence, as a rule, it is better to express even a negative in positive form.

not honest	dishonest
not important	trifling
did not remember	forgot
did not pay any attention to	ignored
did not have much confidence in	distrusted

The antithesis of negative and positive is strong:

Not charity, but simple justice.
Not that I loved Caesar less, but that I loved Rome more.

Negative words other than *not* are usually strong:

The sun never sets upon the British flag.

➤ EXERCISE 13.1: Omitting *Not*

Rewrite the following sentences where appropriate.

1. She did not remember to pay her phone bill.

_____

_____

2. She did not listen to her college professor's recommendation that she review her calculus notes every day.

_____

_____

3. There are not enough research studies on environmental communication.

_____

_____

4. That response is not accurate. _____

_____

_____

5. Please do not hesitate to contact me if you need to. _____

_____

_____

6. We do not have enough solid information to make a decision. _____

_____

_____

7. I am not persuaded that the cause is valid. _____

_____

_____

8. The reports are not complete and we cannot offer a valid assessment at this time. _

_____

_____

14. Use definite, specific, concrete language.

Prefer the specific to the general, the definite to the vague, the concrete to the abstract.

A period of unfavorable weather set in.	It rained every day for a week.
He showed satisfaction as he took possession of his well-earned reward.	He grinned as he pocketed the coin.
There is a general agreement among those who have enjoyed the experience that surfing is productive of great exhilaration.	Generally, those who enjoy surfing find it most exhilarating.

If those who have studied the art of writing are in accord on any one point, it is on this: the surest method of arousing and holding the attention of the reader is by being specific, definite, and concrete. Critics have pointed out how much of the effectiveness of the greatest writers—Homer, Dante, Shakespeare—results from their use of definite and concrete language. John Greenleaf Whittier, a poet and abolitionist, affords many striking examples. Take, for instance, the lines from *Snow-Bound*:

Shut in from all the world without,
We sat the clean-winged hearth about,
Content to let the north-wind roar
In baffled rage at pane and door,
While the red logs before us beat
The frost-line back with tropic heat;
And ever, when a louder blast
Shook beam and rafter as it passed,
The merrier up its roaring draught
The great throat of the chimney laughed;
The house-dog on his paws outspread
Laid to the fire his drowsy head,
The cat's dark silhouette on the wall
A couchant tiger's seemed to fall;
And, for the winter fireside meet,
Between the andirons' straddling feet,
The mug of cider simmered slow,
The apples sputtered in a row,
And, close at hand, the basket stood
With nuts from brown October's wood.

Likewise, prose, particularly narrative and descriptive prose, is made vivid by the same means. If the experiences of Sanger Rainsford and of Sherlock Holmes, of Jo March, of Father Brown, have seemed for the moment real to countless readers, if in reading Dickens we have almost the sense of being physically present during the ghostly visit of Jacob Marley, it is because of the definiteness of the details and the concreteness of the terms used. It is not that every detail is given—that would be impossible as well as to no purpose—but that all the significant details are given with such definiteness that the reader, in imagination, can project himself into the scene.

In exposition and in argument, the writer must, likewise, never lose hold upon the concrete, and even when dealing with general principles, the writer must give particular instances of their application, as the following paragraph demonstrates:

> This superiority of specific expressions is clearly due to the effort required to translate words into thoughts. As we do not think in generals, but in particulars—as whenever any class of things is referred to, we represent it to ourselves by calling to mind individual members of it, it follows that when an abstract word is used, the hearer or reader has to choose from mental stock images to associate with the abstract. In doing this, some mental delay arises and consequently some mental force is expended. If, however, by employing a specific term, an appropriate image can immediately be suggested, efficiency is achieved and a more vivid impression produced.

Herbert Spencer, from whose *Philosophy of Style* the preceding paragraph has been adapted, illustrates the importance of concrete detail:

> In proportion as the manners, customs, and amusements of a nation are cruel and barbarous, the regulations of their penal code will be severe.

> In proportion as men delight in battles, bull-fights, and combats of gladiators, will they punish by hanging, burning, and the rack.

➤ **EXERCISE 14.1: Vague to Specific**
  Rewrite the following sentences using specific language.

1. He lived on the mountain in a house under the trees. _____

_____

_____

2. Fruits of the tropics are typically high in nutrients. _____

_____

_____

3. As he was walking down the street, he saw homes to the left and to the right, and

    some trees. _____

_____

_____

4. She really likes to travel because it helps her understand people better. _____

_____

_____

5. Punishments for breaking laws in some countries are very severe. _____

_____

_____

6. She has a beautiful spirit. _____

_____

_____

7. My home town is surrounded by beautiful scenery. _____

_____

_____

15. Omit needless words.

Vigorous writing is concise. A sentence should contain no unnecessary words—a paragraph no unnecessary sentences—for the same reason that a drawing should have no unnecessary lines and a machine no unnecessary parts. This requires not that the writer make all sentences short, or avoid all detail and treat subjects only in outline, but that the writer make every word tell.

Many expressions in common use violate this principle:

the question as to whether	whether (the question whether)
there is no doubt but that	no doubt (doubtless)
used for fuel purposes	used for fuel
he is a man who	he
in a hasty manner	hastily
this is a subject which	this subject
His story is a strange one.	His story is strange.

The expression *the fact that* is especially unnecessary and should be revised out of every sentence in which it occurs.

owing to the fact that	since (because)
in spite of the fact that	though (although)
call your attention to the fact that	remind you (notify you)
I was unaware of the fact that	I was unaware that (did not know)
the fact that he had not succeeded	his failure
the fact that I had arrived	my arrival

Who is, *which was*, and the like are often superfluous.

His brother, who is a member of the same firm	His brother, a member of the same firm
Trafalgar, which was Nelson's last battle	Trafalgar, Nelson's last battle

As a positive statement is more concise than a negative, and the active voice more concise than the passive, many of the examples given under Rules 12 and 13 illustrate this rule as well.

A common violation of conciseness is the presentation of a single complex idea, step by step, in a series of sentences or independent clauses that might be combined into one.

Macbeth was very ambitious. This led him to wish to become king of Scotland. The witches told him that this wish of his would come true. The king of Scotland at this time was Duncan. Encouraged by his wife, Macbeth murdered Duncan. He was thus enabled to succeed Duncan as king. (51 words)

Encouraged by his wife, Macbeth achieved his ambition and realized the prediction of the witches by murdering Duncan and becoming king of Scotland in his place. (26 words)

➤ **EXERCISE 15.1: Conciseness**
Rewrite the following sentences, omitting unnecessary words. Make other changes as necessary.

1. For the very simple reason that he was stubborn, he refused to go. _____

    _____

    _____

2. The sentence by which the paragraph is begun is awkward. _____

    _____

    _____

3. Whether or not one might decide that following the rules is a good idea, sometimes

    penalties for breaking them are severe. _____

    _____

    _____

4. Owing to the simple fact that airfares tend to be slightly lower in October, that is

    the time during which we have planned our vacation. _____

    _____

    _____

5. There isn't a lot known about most things in this day and age just yet, but scientists

    keep working at it, either discrediting what once was considered solid knowledge or

    building on it and advancing that knowledge. _____

    _____

    _____

    _____

    _____

16. Avoid a succession of loose sentences.

One method of varying sentences is through the use of loose and periodic sentences. A *loose sentence* is one in which the various parts—subject, predicate, modifier, etc.—occur in the order that they naturally suggest themselves to the mind. A *periodic sentence* is one in which the parts are so arranged that the sense is incomplete until the end is reached.

The following are examples of loose and periodic sentences:

LOOSE	PERIODIC
None but the fittest survive in the great struggle for existence.	In the great struggle for existence, none but the fittest survive.
The modern system of technical education renders inestimable aid to men not only in engineering but also in the ranks of the liberal professions.	To men not only in engineering but also in the ranks of the liberal professions, the modern system of technical education renders inestimable aid.

This rule refers especially to loose sentences of a particular type, those consisting of two coordinate clauses, the second introduced by a conjunction or relative. Although single sentences of this type may be common and useful, a series soon becomes monotonous and tedious.

In general, the loose sentence is easier to construct and easier to understand than the periodic sentence, simply because it follows the order in which the words naturally occur to a person, when a writer thinks of what she wishes to say and not of the form of expression. For this reason, the loose sentence is especially adapted to conversation and letter writing. Periodic sentences are appropriate for stately and formal composition.

An unskilled writer will sometimes construct a whole paragraph of loose sentences, using as connectives *and*, *but*, *so*, and less frequently, *who*, *which*, *when*, *where*, and *while*, these last in nonrestrictive senses (See Rule 3.)

> The third concert of the subscription series was given last evening, and a large audience was in attendance. Mr. Edward Appleton was the soloist, and the Boston Symphony Orchestra furnished the instrumental music. The former showed himself to be an artist of the first rank, while the latter proved itself fully deserving of its high reputation. The interest aroused by the series has been very gratifying to the Committee, and it is planned to give a similar series annually hereafter. The fourth concert will be given on Tuesday, May 10, when an equally attractive program will be presented.

Apart from its triteness and emptiness, the previous paragraph is weak because of the structure of its sentences, with their mechanical symmetry and sing-song rhythm. Contrast them with the sentences in the paragraph below.

Unjust laws exist: shall we be content to obey them, or shall we endeavor to amend them, and obey them until we have succeeded, or shall we transgress them at once? Men generally, under such a government as this, think that they ought to wait until they have persuaded the majority to alter them. They think that, if they should resist, the remedy would be worse than the evil. But it is the fault of the government itself that the remedy is worse than the evil. *It* makes it worse. Why is it not more apt to anticipate and provide for reform? Why does it not cherish its wise minority? Why does it cry and resist before it is hurt? Why does it not encourage its citizens to be on the alert to point out its faults, and *do* better than it would have them? Why does it always crucify Christ, and excommunicate Copernicus and Luther, and pronounce Washington and Franklin rebels?

—Henry David Thoreau, "Civil Disobedience"

The principle of suspense makes the periodic sentence more emphatic than the loose sentence; hence, for the sake of variety and force, it is advisable to use occasionally the periodic form, provided the sentence is so short and simple that the reader can grasp the meaning at once.

➢ **EXERCISE 16.1: Loose and Periodic Sentences**
   Rewrite the following loose sentences to become periodic sentences.

1. She awaited her death in the passageway behind the courthouse. _____

   _____

   _____

2. The hurricane destroyed everything in its path, even though we were fairly certain

   we would be spared damage due to solid, state-of-the-art residential construction.

   _____

   _____

3. Darian moved to the tropics because he lost his professional job and was looking for

   a new career. _____

   _____

   _____

4. The accident occurred at midnight on a solitary road to nowhere. _____

_____

_____

5. The ship sank on its maiden voyage. _____

_____

_____

> **EXERCISE 16.2: Emphasis**
> Rewrite the following sentences so that the most prominent idea receives the most emphasis possible. Make other changes as necessary.

1. Owing to one great surfer, this beach will always be protected. _____

_____

2. Those two guys caught 52 crabs out there in the boat that day. _____

_____

_____

3. The fire took out 37 homes all along the ridge, causing great distress to all of these families and indeed the entire neighborhood. _____

_____

_____

4. In a hammock is probably the best way for a lot of people to spend their vacations.

_____

_____

5. You ordered him to death while the sacred words, "I am a Roman citizen," were on his lips._____

_____

_____

6. Without warning, the volcano erupted, disrupting the vacations of thousands of travelers. _____

_____

_____

7. I shall not vote for this measure, unless it is clearly constitutional. _____

_____

_____

8. He feared when there was no danger, and he wept when there was no sorrow. ___

_____

_____

9. Greene was the ablest commander in the Revolutionary War, next to Washington.

_____

_____

10. Much veganism is rooted in the idea that animal consumption contributes to the world's largest problems. _____

_____

_____

17. Express co-ordinate ideas in similar form.

This principle, that of parallel construction, requires that expressions of similar content and function should be outwardly similar. The likeness of form enables the reader to recognize more readily the likeness of content and function. Familiar instances from the Bible are the Ten Commandments, the Beatitudes, and the petitions of the Lord's Prayer.

The unskillful writer often violates this principle from a mistaken belief that she should constantly vary the form of expressions. It is true that in repeating a statement for emphasis, the writer may have need to vary its form. But apart from this, she should follow the principle of parallel construction.

Formerly, science was taught by the textbook method, while now the laboratory method is employed.	Formerly, science was taught by the textbook method; now it is taught by the laboratory method.

The left-hand version gives the impression that the writer is undecided or timid; the writer seems unable or afraid to choose one form of expression and hold to it. The right-hand version shows that the writer has at least made a choice and abided by it.

Applying this principle, an article or a preposition applying to all the members of a series must either be used only before the first term or else be repeated before each term.

The French, the Italians, Spanish, and Portuguese	The French, the Italians, the Spanish, and the Portuguese
In spring, summer, or in winter	In spring, summer, or winter
	(In spring, in summer, or in winter)

Correlative expressions (*both, and*; *not, but*; *not only, but also*; *either, or*; *first, second, third*; and the like) should be followed by the same grammatical construction, that is, virtually, by the same part of speech. (Such combinations as "both Henry and I," "not silk, but a cheap substitute," are obviously within the rule.) Many violations of this rule (as the first three following examples) arise from faulty arrangement—others (as the last following example) from the use of unlike constructions.

It was both a long ceremony and very tedious.	The ceremony was both long and tedious.
A time not for words but action.	A time not for words but for action.
Either you must grant his request or incur his ill will.	You must either grant his request or incur his ill will.
My objections are, first, the injustice of the measure; second, that it is unconstitutional.	My objections are, first, that the measure is unjust; second, that it is unconstitutional.

It may be asked, what if a writer needs to express a very large number of similar ideas, say 20? Must the 20 consecutive sentences be of the same pattern? On closer examination, the student will probably find that the difficulty is imaginary, that the 20 ideas can be classified in groups, and that the principle need only be applied within each group. Otherwise, the writer should avoid difficulty by putting the large number of statements into a table.

> ➤ **EXERCISE 17.1: Parallel Structure**
> Underline the phrases in the following sentences that need to be made parallel. Then rewrite the sentences to make these phrases parallel.

Example: He is a man <u>of large ideas</u> and <u>having firm principles</u>.

Answer: He is a man of large ideas and firm principles.

1. In his right hand was the American flag, and he held in his left a tattered Spanish ensign.

_____

_____

2. After having completed the undertaking, and when he had begun another, he felt that his success was assured.

_____

_____

3. Dinner was served in a spacious hall, the panels of which shone with wax, and with the casings hung with ivy.

_____

_____

4. In one direction rolled a train of wagons, and a company of soldiers was marching in the other.

_____

_____

5. A large market place was in the center, with the council house at the side.

_____

_____

6. By day Penelope wove the wondrous web; she unraveled her work when it was dark.

_____

_____

7. The mob determined to capture the king, imprison him, and then, at the last, they would try him for his life.

_____

_____

8. Cooper wrote stories of action and adventure; the works of Hawthorne are weird and strange.

_____

_____

9. They were of one generation, and he had been brought up in another.

_____

_____

10. The first boy accepted the generous offer, but the second thought it best not to agree.

_____

_____

11. He enjoyed listening to others, but others paid no attention when he spoke.

_____

_____

18. Keep related words together.

In English, the position of the words in a sentence is the principal means of showing their relationship. The writer must, therefore, bring together the words, and groups of words, that are related in thought, and keep apart those that are not so related.

The subject of a sentence and the principal verb should not, as a rule, be separated by a phrase or clause that can be transferred to the beginning.

Wordsworth, in the fifth book of *The Excursion*, gives a detailed description of this church.	In the fifth book of *The Excursion*, Wordsworth gives a detailed description of this church.
Cast iron, when treated in a Bessemer converter, is changed into steel.	By treatment in a Bessemer converter, cast iron is changed into steel.

The objection is that the interposed phrase or clause needlessly interrupts the natural order of the main clause. Usually, however, this objection does not hold when the order is interrupted only by a relative clause or by an expression in apposition. Nor does it hold in periodic sentences in which the interruption is a deliberately used means of creating suspense (See Rule 20).

The relative pronoun should come, as a rule, immediately after its antecedent. An *antecedent* is the noun or pronoun to which the relative pronoun refers. A **relative pronoun** is a type of pronoun that introduces a dependent or relative clause.

There was a *look* in his eye **that** boded mischief.	In his eye was a *look* **that** boded mischief.
This is a portrait of *Benjamin Harrison*, grandson of William Henry Harrison, **who** became President in 1889.	This is a portrait of *Benjamin Harrison*, **who** became President in 1889. He was the grandson of William Henry Harrison.

If the antecedent consists of a group of words, the relative comes at the end of the group, unless this would cause ambiguity.

They offered a proposal to amend the Sherman Act, which has been variously judged.	They offered a proposal, which has been variously judged, to amend the Sherman Act.

They offered a proposal to amend the much-debated Sherman Act. |
| The grandson of William Henry Harrison, who. | William Henry Harrison's grandson, who |

A noun in apposition may come between the antecedent and relative because in such a combination, no real ambiguity can arise.

The Duke of York, his brother, who was regarded with hostility by the Whigs . . .

Modifiers should come, if possible, next to the word they modify. If several expressions modify the same word, they should be so arranged that no wrong relation is suggested.

All the members were not present.	Not all the members were present.
He only found two mistakes.	He found only two mistakes.
Major R. E. Joyce will give a lecture on Tuesday evening in Bailey Hall, to which the public is invited, on "My Experiences in Mesopotamia" at eight p.m.	On Tuesday evening at eight p.m., Major R. E. Joyce will give a lecture in Bailey Hall on "My Experiences in Mesopotamia." The public is invited.

> **EXERCISE 18.1: Modifiers, Ambiguity, and Conciseness**
> Rewrite the sentences, moving phrases as necessary, to reduce ambiguity and increase clarity.

1. The damage to the car amounted to $1,200, which was caused by the accident.

   _____

   _____

2. So many species are declining that it's alarming because of human behavior. _____

   _____

   _____

3. Sea turtles won't come to bright beaches which return to their birthplace beaches

   to nest. _____

   _____

   _____

4. The man greeted me driving the car. _____

   _____

5. Traveling abroad has many advantages with his brother. _____

   _____

6. The idea of working late has infiltrated into many industrialized societies, an

   American value. _____

   _____

   _____

7. The suicide rate among professionals is alarming, especially with dentists. _____

   _____

   _____

   _____

8. The banking industry profits from every war and every social downturn, an industry only ostensibly there to help the people. _____

_____

_____

9. Judge Harrison ruled against the juvenile defendant, sentencing him by the adult card, John's brother. _____

_____

_____

10. With appositives, writing sentences such as these isn't as easy as it looks. _____

_____

_____

19. In summaries, keep to one tense.

In summarizing the action of a drama, the writer should always use the present tense. In summarizing a poem, story, or novel, writers should also use the present, though they may use the past if preferred. If the summary is in the present tense, antecedent action should be expressed by the perfect; if in the past, by the past perfect.

> An unforeseen chance prevents Friar John from delivering Friar Lawrence's letter to Romeo. Meanwhile, owing to her father's arbitrary change of the day set for her wedding, Juliet *has been compelled* to drink the potion on Tuesday night, with the result that Balthasar informs Romeo of her supposed death before Friar Lawrence learns of the non-delivery of the letter.

But whichever tense is used in the summary, a past tense in indirect discourse or in indirect question remains unchanged.

> The Friar confesses that it was he who married them.

Apart from the exceptions noted, whichever tense the writer chooses, he should use throughout. Shifting from one tense to the other gives the appearance of uncertainty and irresolution.

In presenting the statements or the thought of someone else, as in summarizing an essay or reporting a speech, the writer should avoid overusing such expressions as "he said," "he stated," "the speaker added," "the speaker then went on to say," "the author also thinks," or the like. The writer should indicate clearly at the outset, once for all, that what follows is summary, and then waste no words in repeating the notification.

In notebooks, in newspapers, and in handbooks of literature, summaries of one kind or another may be indispensable, and for young children it is a useful exercise to retell a story in their own words. But in the criticism or interpretation of literature, the writer should be careful to avoid dropping into summary. Writers may find it necessary to devote one or two sentences to indicating the subject, or the opening situation, of the work they are discussing. They may cite numerous details to illustrate its qualities; however, they should aim to write commentary supported by evidence, not a summary with occasional comment. Similarly, if the scope of the discussion includes a number of works, they will generally do better not to discuss each work singly in chronological order, but instead to aim from the beginning at establishing general conclusions.

Writing with the Perfect

See that the verbs in your sentence are in proper tense sequence. The main verb in a sentence sets the time, to which the subordinate verbs must be correctly related. If the subordinate verb expresses time before or after the time of the main verb, this difference in time must be indicated.

Indicate action recently completed at the present time by the perfect.

> He *feels* (present) that he *has been injured* (perfect).

Indicate action completed before some definite time in the past by the past perfect.

> Last night, he *realized* (past) that he *had been injured* (past perfect) **at last week's game**.
> I *admired* (past) the etchings that he *had bought* (past perfect) **on his vacation**.

When using the past and past perfect in the same context, you must ensure that the difference in time between that expressed by the main verb and that expressed by the subordinate verb is clearly evident. This can be done through the use of adverbial phrases or clauses or through the context of your writing.

The past perfect includes the past tense of "to have" (had) plus the past participle of the verb.

> **EXERCISE 19.1: Writing with the Past Perfect**
> For each statement below, finish the sentence by adding a clause written in the past perfect and by adding a word, phrase, or clause that indicates the difference in time. (Answers will vary.)

Example: He *realized* that.
            He realized <u>that he had been injured</u> **at last week's game**.
Example: The girls and boys jumped from their seats.
Example: Because their <u>names had been called</u>, the girls and boys jumped from their seats.

1. They took their coats.

   _____

   _____

2. Little Red Riding Hood stared at her grandmother's teeth.

   _____

   _____

3. Brutus supported the assassination of Caesar.

   _____

   _____

4. Cinderella's carriage turned back into a pumpkin.

   _____

   _____

5. Our current leader cried.

   _____

   _____

6. She graduated from the university.

   _____

   _____

7. His money was gone.

   _____

   _____

1. The evidence proved that the attacker had broken into the house before midnight.

_____

_____

2. After babysitting his younger brothers, Steven realized he had forgotten to do his homework.

_____

_____

3. By the time he graduated from high school, he had started a business and written a novel.

_____

_____

4. Little Red Riding Hood stared at her grandmother's teeth, which had changed significantly since her last visit.

_____

_____

EXERCISE 19.3. Tense

On the following page, rewrite the passage from Edgar Allen Poe's "The Devil in the Belfry" so that it is in the present tense. Change the verb tenses as appropriate.

Notwithstanding the obscurity which thus enveloped the date of the foundation of Vondervotteimittis, and the derivation of its name, there can be no doubt, as I say before, that it had always existed as we find it at this epoch. The oldest man in the borough could remember not the slightest difference in the appearance of any portion of it; and, indeed, the very suggestion of such a possibility is considered an insult. The site of the village is in a perfectly circular valley, about a quarter of a mile in circumference, and entirely surrounded by gentle hills, over whose summit the people had never yet ventured to pass. For this they assigned the very good reason that they do not believe there is anything at all on the other side.

20. Place the emphatic words of a sentence at the end.

The proper place in the sentence for the word, or group of words, that the writer desires to make most prominent is usually the end.

Humanity has hardly advanced in fortitude since that time, though it has advanced in many other ways.	Since that time, humanity has advanced in many other ways, but it has hardly advanced in fortitude.
This steel is principally used for making razors, because of its hardness.	Because of its hardness, this steel is principally used in making razors.

The word or group of words entitled to this position of prominence is usually the logical predicate—that is, the new element in the sentence, as it is in the second example.

The effectiveness of the periodic sentence arises from the prominence that it gives to the main statement.

> Four centuries ago, Christopher Columbus, one of the Italian mariners whom the decline of their own republics had put at the service of the world and of adventure, seeking for Spain a westward passage to the Indies as a set-off against the achievements of Portuguese discoverers, lighted on America.

> With these hopes and in this belief I would urge you, laying aside all hindrance, thrusting away all private aims, to devote yourself unswervingly and unflinchingly to the vigorous and successful prosecution of this war.

The other prominent position in the sentence is the beginning. Any element in the sentence, other than the subject, may become emphatic when placed first.

> Deceit or treachery he could never forgive.
> Vast and rude, fretted by the action of nearly three thousand years, the fragments of this architecture may often seem, at first sight, like works of nature.

A subject coming first in its sentence may be emphatic, but hardly by its position alone. In the sentence,

> Great kings worshipped at his shrine.

The emphasis upon *kings* arises largely from its meaning and from the context. To receive special emphasis, the subject of a sentence must take the position of the predicate.

> Through the middle of the valley flowed a winding stream.

The principle that the proper place for what is to be made most prominent is the end applies equally to the words of a sentence, to the sentences of a paragraph, and to the paragraphs of a composition.

➢ **EXERCISE 20.1: Emphatic Sentences**
Render each of these sentences more emphatic by rearranging the words so that the word or words to be emphasized are located at the beginning or end of the sentence. Make other changes as necessary.

1. Brave Horatius then spake out.

_____

_____

2. The whip goes crack and we go off.

_____

_____

3. Earth praises God with her thousand voices.

_____

_____

4. A thing of beauty is forever a joy.

_____

_____

5. The rebel rides no more on his raids.

_____

_____

6. The principal thing is wisdom; therefore get wisdom.

_____

_____

7. He did well whatever he did.

_____

_____

8. You are a snob if you are ashamed of your poverty and blush for your calling.

_____

_____

9. A gale wind from the north blew colder and louder.

_____

_____

Note: The usual order of an English sentence is as follows: adjectives modifying the subject, subject, adjective phrase or clause, verb, adverb, or adverbial phrase or clause, and object or other complement with its modifiers. Any change in this arrangement at once attracts the reader's attention and centers interest on the element out of its usual position.

Example of varied emphasis,

1. A beautiful girl in a bright red dress stood before him.
2. A girl, beautiful, in a bright red dress, stood before him.
3. In a bright red dress, a beautiful girl stood before him.
4. Before him stood a beautiful girl in a bright red dress.
5. Before him a beautiful girl in a bright red dress stood absolutely still.
6. There stood before him a beautiful girl in a bright red dress.

This device must, however, be used sparingly. It is most natural when the writer or speaker is moved by strong feeling. For this reason, as well as from the demands of rhythm, it is more often found in poetry. Any attempt to use it frequently or to make a forced use of it tends to give at once the impression of artificiality:

Flung he then upon the tiled floor his worse than useless fountain pen.

➢ **EXERCISE 20.2: Creating Emphasis**
Rewrite each of the given sentences five different ways. Change the sentence arrangement so that a different element of the sentence is emphasized. Follow the example of varied emphasis on the previous page. (Answers will vary.)

1. As I looked I saw a flame shoot up from the building.

_____

_____

_____

_____

_____

_____

_____

_____

_____

_____

2. After a fierce struggle, Beowulf slew the monster Grendel.

_____

_____

_____

_____

_____

_____

_____

_____

_____

_____

3. She saw a horse running down the street and immediately hurried after him.

_____

_____

_____

_____

_____

_____

_____

_____

_____

4. Brom Bones succeeded in scaring Ichabod Crane out of Sleepy Hollow.

_____

_____

_____

_____

_____

_____

_____

_____

_____

5. David with his sling and a pebble slew the Philistine giant.

_____

_____

_____

_____

_____

_____

_____

_____

_____

_____

6. As Farmer Brown was going uphill yesterday with a load of apples, the rear board of his wagon broke.

_____

_____

_____

_____

_____

_____

_____

_____

_____

_____

7. Jane fell into the creek last week.

_____

_____

_____

_____

_____

_____

_____

_____

_____

_____

21. Imitating the Masters of Literature

Adapted from "Composition and Writing" by Noah Webster.

Composition in writing is the formation of sentences for the expression of ideas.

Style is the manner in which sentences are composed and arranged. Every writer has a manner, and generally a peculiar manner, of expressing ideas, which forms style.

Styles are of several kinds or characters. The more common characteristics of style are force, vehemence, elegance, brevity, copiousness or diffusiveness, precision, neatness, looseness, feebleness, and plainness.

The Forcible Style

The *forcible* style consists in the use of bold, strong words and phrases, adapted to exhibit striking images; and the omission of small unimportant words. It is plain, direct, strong, and convincing, and implies good intellectual powers, and a well-disciplined mind.

Consider the following,

> What must I do, is all that concerns me, not what the people think. This rule, equally arduous in actual and in intellectual life, may serve for the whole distinction between greatness and meanness. It is the harder because you will always find those who think they know what is your duty better than you know it. It is easy in the world to live after the world's opinion; it is easy in solitude to live after our own; but the great man is he who in the midst of the crowd keeps with perfect sweetness the independence of solitude.

> —Ralph Waldo Emerson

➢ **EXERCISE 21.1: Style Practice**
Complete Steps 1 and 2 (or Steps 1 and 3) of the writing options below. Advanced students will want to complete all steps. **Using the Checklist** located on page 183, correct your imitation. **Compare your writing** to the original passage. Were you able to imitate the style of the original passage? **Identify areas** in which your writing needs improvement. Identify areas in which you have bettered the original author.

Step 1: Read the forcible model closely. Copy the model on the lines provided. By simply rewriting the model, you will become more familiar with the style of the author.

Step 2: To further evaluate the author's style, write a brief outline to help you remember the content of the passage. When you are finished, put away the original model. Using your outline, rewrite the passage, maintaining the author's original style.

Step 3: Change the topic and create your own passage imitating the style of the original passage. (Suggested topics: For a new topic, refer to Benjamin Franklin's 13 Virtues on page 185.)

The Vehement Style

A *vehement* style is characterized by the use of words expressive of earnestness or feeling, and so arranged as to excite a rapid succession of ideas. This style expresses a greater degree of excitement, and a deeper current of feeling than the forcible style.

Consider the following,

> Besides, Sir, we shall not fight our battles alone. There is a just God, that presides over the destinies of nations, and will raise up friends to fight our battles for us. The battle, Sir, is not to the strong alone: it is to the vigilant; the active; the brave! Besides, Sir, we have no choice. Though we were base enough to desire it; it is now too late to retire from the contest. There is no retreat but in submission and slavery! Our chains are forged! Their clanking may be heard on the plains of Boston! The war is inevitable; and let it come! I repeat it, Sir; let it come!

> It is in vain to extenuate the matter. Gentlemen may cry, peace! peace! but there is no peace. The war is actually begun. The next gale that shall sweep from the North will bring to our ears the clash of resounding arms! Our brethren are already in the field! Why stand we here idle? What is it that gentlemen wish? What would they have? Is life so dear; are chains so sweet, as to be purchased at the price of chains and slavery? Forbid it, Almighty God! I know not what course others may take; but as for myself, give me Liberty! Or give me Death!

> —Patrick Henry, "Give Me Liberty, or Give Me Death!"

> ➤ **EXERCISE 21.2: Style Practice**
> **Complete Steps** 1 and 2 (or Steps 1 and 3) of the writing options below. Advanced students will want to complete all steps. **Using the Checklist** located on page 183, correct your imitation. **Compare your writing** to the original passage. Were you able to imitate the style of the original passage? **Identify areas** in which your writing needs improvement. Identify areas in which you have bettered the original author.

Step 1: Read the model closely. Copy the model on the lines provided. By simply rewriting the model, you will become more intimately familiar with the vehement style.

Step 2: To further evaluate the author's style, write a brief outline to help you remember the content of the passage. When you are finished, put away the original model. Using your outline, rewrite the passage, maintaining the author's original style.

Step 3: Change the topic and create your own passage in the vehement style. (Suggested topics: Choose a social topic about which you are passionate—the death penalty, gun control, a current war)

The Elegant Style

Elegance consists in the use of the most proper words, and a smooth natural arrangement of all the parts of sentences. "An elegant writer," says Blair, "is one who pleases the fancy and the ear, while he informs the understanding; and who gives us his ideas clothed with all the beauty of expression, but not overcharged with any of its misplaced finery."

Consider the following,

> He who, in an enlightened and literary society, aspires to be a great poet must first become a little child; he must take to pieces the whole web of his mind. He must unlearn much of that knowledge which has perhaps constituted hitherto his chief title to superiority. His very talents will be a hindrance to him. His difficulties will be proportioned to his proficiency in the pursuits which are fashionable among his contemporaries; and that proficiency will in general be proportioned to the vigour and activity of his mind. And it is well if, after all his sacrifices and exertions, his works do not resemble a lisping man or a modern ruin.

—Thomas Babington Macaulay, *The Greatest Works of the Greatest Authors*

> ➢ **EXERCISE 21.3: Style Practice**
> **Complete Steps** 1 and 2 (or Steps 1 and 3) of the writing options below. Advanced students will want to complete all steps. **Using the Checklist** located on page 183, correct your imitation. **Compare your writing** to the original passage. Were you able to imitate the style of the original passage? **Identify areas** in which your writing needs improvement. Identify areas in which you have bettered the original author.

Step 1: Read the model closely. Copy the model on the lines provided. By simply rewriting the model, you will become more intimately familiar with the style of the author.

Step 2: To further evaluate the author's style, write a brief outline to help you remember the content of the passage. When you are finished, put away the original model. Using your outline, rewrite the passage, maintaining the author's original style.

Step 3: Change the topic and create your own passage imitating the style of the original passage. (Suggested topics: To find a new topic, fill in the blanks below.)

- To be financially independent, one must _____.
- To be content in life, one must _____.
- To be a leader, one must _____.
- To acquire wisdom and understanding, one must _____.

The Brief Style

Brevity consists in the use of few words to express the ideas intended. It is a concise style, short, pithy, and bold. In use, the short sentence is well suited for definitions, for propositions, and for transitions of thought. And as at times when the mind is under a stress of strong feeling, or the action of a story is rapid, short sentences serve best.

Consider the following,

> Tell General Howard I know his heart. I am tired of fighting. Our chiefs are killed. Looking Glass is dead. Too-hul-hul-Shute is dead. The old men are all dead. It is the young men who say yes or no. He who led on the young men is dead. It is cold and we have no blankets. The little children are freezing to death. My people, some of them, have run away to the hills, and have no blankets, no food; no one knows where they are—perhaps freezing to death. I want to have time to look for my children and see how many of them I can find. Maybe I shall find them among the dead. Hear me, my chiefs. I am tired; my heart is sick and sad. From where the sun now stands I will fight no more forever.

— Chief Joseph's Surrender Speech, 1877

> ➤ **EXERCISE 21.4: Style Practice**
> **Complete Steps** 1 and 2 (or Steps 1 and 3) of the writing options below. Advanced students will want to complete all steps. **Using the Checklist** located on page 183, correct your imitation. **Compare your writing** to the original passage. Were you able to imitate the style of the original passage? **Identify areas** in which your writing needs improvement. Identify areas in which you have bettered the original author.

Step 1: Read the model closely. Copy the model on the lines provided. By simply rewriting the model, you will become more intimately familiar with the style of the author.

Step 2: To further evaluate the author's style, write a brief outline to help you remember the content of the passage. When you are finished, put away the original model. Using your outline, rewrite the passage, maintaining the author's original style.

Step 3: Change the topic and create your own passage imitating the style of the original passage. (Suggested topics: To find a new topic, complete the sentence below. Choose a topic that evokes strong feelings.)

I am tired of _____.

The Precise Style

Precision consists in the use of as few words as the clear expression of ideas will allow, and a freedom from all superfluous words, together with a lucid arrangement of words, phrases, and clauses. George MacDonald, the mentor to Lewis Carroll, author of *Alice in Wonderland*, demonstrates a precise writing style as he explains how a person may become a good writer.

> "If a man has anything to say he will manage to say it; if he has nothing to communicate, there is no reason why he should have a good style any more than why he should have a good purse without any money, or a good scabbard without any sword. For my part I always scorned the very idea of forming a style. Every true man with anything to say has a style of his own, which, for its development requires only common sense. In the first place, he must see that he has said what he means; in the next, that he has not said it so that it may be mistaken for what he does not mean. The mere moving of a word to another place may help to prevent such mistake. Then he must remove what is superfluous, what is unnecessary or unhelpful to the understanding of his meaning. He must remove whatever obscures or dulls the meaning, and makes it necessary to search for what might have been plainly understood at once. All this implies a combination of writer and critic, not often found. Whatever, in a word, seems to the writer himself objectionable, either in regard to sense or sound, he must rigorously remove. He must use no phrase because it sounds fine, and no imagined ornament which does not contribute to the sense or the feeling of what he writes."

— George MacDonald, *The Writer's Book*

> ➤ **EXERCISE 21.5: Style Practice**
> **Complete Steps** 1 and 2 (or Steps 1 and 3) of the writing options below. Advanced students will want to complete all steps. **Using the Checklist** located on page 183, correct your imitation. **Compare your writing** to the original passage. Were you able to imitate the style of the original passage? **Identify areas** in which your writing needs improvement. Identify areas in which you have bettered the original author.

Step 1: Read the model closely. Copy the model on the lines provided. By simply rewriting the model, you will become more intimately familiar with the style of the author.

Step 2: To further evaluate the author's style, write a brief outline to help you remember the content of the passage. When you are finished, put away the original model. Using your outline, rewrite the passage, maintaining the author's original style.

Step 3: Change the topic and create your own passage imitating the style of the original passage. (Suggested topic: If a person avoids challenges, she avoids the opportunity to learn.)

The Copious Style

Copiousness consists in the use of all the words and phrases necessary for a full expression of all the material ideas the writer intends to communicate.

It (the guillotine) seems as though it were a being, possessed of I know not what somber initiative; one would say that this piece of carpenter's work saw, that this machine heard, that this mechanism understood, that this wood, this iron, and these cords were possessed of will. In the frightful meditation into which its presence casts the soul, the scaffold appears in terrible guise, and as though taking part in what is going on. The scaffold is the accomplice of the executioner; it devours, it eats flesh, it drinks blood; the scaffold is a sort of monster fabricated by the judge and the carpenter, a spectre which seems to live with a horrible vitality composed of all the death which it has inflicted.

— Victor Hugo, *Les Misérables*

➢ **EXERCISE 21.6: Style Practice**
Complete Steps 1 and 2 (or Steps 1 and 3) of the writing options below. Advanced students will want to complete all steps. **Using the Checklist** located on page 183, correct your imitation. **Compare your writing** to the original passage. Were you able to imitate the style of the original passage? **Identify areas** in which your writing needs improvement. Identify areas in which you have bettered the original author.

Step 1: Read the model closely. Copy the model on the lines provided. By simply rewriting the model, you will become more intimately familiar with the style of the author.

Step 2: To further evaluate the author's style, write a brief outline to help you remember the content of the passage. When you are finished, put away the original model. Using your outline, rewrite the passage, maintaining the author's original style.

Step 3: Change the topic and create your own passage imitating the style of the original. (Suggested topics: Personify a non-living item. Pick one from the list below, or think of a new one. Begin your passage with: It _____ seems as though . . .)

microwave	pool	oven	coffee maker	automobile
train	airplane	tractor	basketball goal	government
river	mountain	tree	garbage	computer

The Diffuse Style

Diffusiveness is allied to copiousness, but it may include the use of superfluous words and phrases. The sentences tend to be long and verbose, and contain many and varied illustrations.

Simon Wheeler backed me into a corner and blockaded me there with his chair, and then sat me down and reeled off the monotonous narrative which follows this paragraph. He never smiled, he never frowned, he never changed his voice from the gentle-flowing key to which he tuned the initial sentence, he never betrayed the slightest suspicion of enthusiasm; but all through the interminable narrative there ran a vein of impressive earnestness and sincerity, which showed me plainly that, so far from his imagining that there was anything ridiculous or funny about his story, he regarded it as a really important matter, and admired its two heroes as men of transcendent genius in *finesse*. To me, the spectacle of a man drifting serenely along through such a queer yarn without ever smiling, was exquisitely absurd. As I said before, I asked him to tell me what he knew of Rev. Leonidas W. Smiley, and he replied as follows. I let him go on in his own way, and never interrupted him once:

There was a feller here once by the name of *Jim* Smiley, in the winter of '49—or maybe it was the spring of '50—I don't recollect exactly, somehow, though what makes me think it was one or the other is because I remember the big flume wasn't finished when he first came to the camp; but any way he was the curiosest man about always betting on anything that turned up you ever see, if he could get anybody to bet on the other side; and if he couldn't, he'd change sides. Any way that suited the other man would suit him—any way just so's he got a bet, *he* was satisfied. But still he was lucky, uncommon lucky; he most always come out winner. He was always ready and laying for a chance; there couldn't be no solit'ry thing mentioned but that feller'd offer to bet on it, and take any side you please, as I was just telling you. If there was a horse-race, you'd find him flush, or you'd find him busted at the end of it; if there was a dog-fight, he'd bet on it; if there was a cat-fight, he'd bet on it; if there was a chicken-fight, he'd bet on it; why, if there was two birds sitting on a fence, he would bet you which one would fly first; or if there was a camp-meeting, he would be there reg'lar, to bet on Parson Walker, which he judged to be the best exhorter about here, and so he was, too, and a good man.

— Mark Twain, "The Celebrated Jumping Frog of Calaveras County"

➤ **EXERCISE 21.7: Style Practice**
Complete Steps 1 and 2 (or Steps 1 and 3) of the writing options below. Advanced students will want to complete all steps. **Using the Checklist** located on page 183, correct your imitation. **Compare your writing** to the original passage. Were you able to imitate the style of the original passage? **Identify areas** in which your writing needs improvement. Identify areas in which you have bettered the original author.

Step 1: Read the model closely. Copy the model on the lines provided. By simply rewriting the model, you will become more intimately familiar with the style of the author.

Step 2: To further evaluate the author's style, write a brief outline to help you remember the content of the passage. When you are finished, put away the original model. Using your outline, rewrite the passage, maintaining the author's original style.

Step 3: Change the topic and create your own passage imitating the style of the original passage. (Suggested topic: Rewrite the passage by Mark Twain, replacing the narrator and Simon Wheeler with two of your favorite characters. One character will be the narrator and will question the other character regarding directions to some place, the location of another character, or the details of an event. The two replacement characters you choose may be from the same story or world, but they do not have to be. Be sure to choose a setting for their conversation.)

_____

_____

_____

_____

_____

_____

_____

_____

_____

_____

_____

_____

_____

The Neat Style

Neatness is allied to brevity and precision, as it excludes the use of superfluous words, and includes a good arrangement of the parts of sentences. This style implies a certain degree of figurative language. The figurative language used, however, is not of the most showy or brilliant kind, but such as is easily attained. A writer who employs this kind of style considers the beauties of language as an object worthy of attention.

In the example below, Susan Glaspell provides an excellent example of neatness. She uses simple words with vivid descriptions, personification, and comparative language to tell the story of a murder investigation.

"Martha!" now came her husband's impatient voice. "Don't keep folks waiting out here in the cold."

She again opened the storm-door, and this time joined the three men and the one woman waiting for her in the big two-seated buggy.

After she had the robes tucked around her she took another look at the woman who sat beside her on the back seat. She had met Mrs. Peters the year before at the county fair, and the thing she remembered about her was that she didn't seem like a sheriff's wife. She was small and thin and didn't have a strong voice. Mrs. Gorman, sheriff's wife before Gorman went out and Peters came in, had a voice that somehow seemed to be backing up the law with every word. But if Mrs. Peters didn't look like a sheriff's wife, Peters made it up in looking like a sheriff. He was to a dot the kind of man who could get himself elected sheriff—a heavy man with a big voice, who was particularly genial with the law-abiding, as if to make it plain that he knew the difference between criminals and non-criminals. And right there it came into Mrs. Hale's mind, with a stab, that this man who was so pleasant and lively with all of them was going to the Wrights' now as a sheriff.

"The country's not very pleasant this time of year," Mrs. Peters at last ventured, as if she felt they ought to be talking as well as the men.

Mrs. Hale scarcely finished her reply, for they had gone up a little hill and could see the Wright place now, and seeing it did not make her feel like talking. It looked very lonesome this cold March morning. It had always been a lonesome-looking place. It was down in a hollow, and the poplar trees around it were lonesome-looking trees. The men were looking at it and talking about what had happened. The county attorney was bending to one side of the buggy, and kept looking steadily at the place as they drew up to it.

"I'm glad you came with me," Mrs. Peters said nervously, as the two women were about to follow the men in through the kitchen door.

—Susan Glaspell, "A Jury of Her Peers"

➢ **EXERCISE 21.8: Style Practice**
Complete Steps 1 and 2 (or Steps 1 and 3) of the writing options below. Advanced students will want to complete all steps. **Using the Checklist** located on page 183, correct your imitation. **Compare your writing** to the original passage. Were you able to imitate the style of the original passage? **Identify areas** in which your writing needs improvement. Identify areas in which you have bettered the original author.

Step 1: Read the bolded paragraph closely. Copy it on the lines provided. By simply rewriting the model, you will become more intimately familiar with the style of the author.

Step 2: To further evaluate the author's style, write a brief outline to help you remember the content of the passage. When you are finished, put away the original model. Using your outline, rewrite the passage, maintaining the author's original style.

Step 3: Change the topic and create your own passage imitating the style of the original passage. (Suggested topic: Rewrite a scene from a familiar narrative—an historical event, a fictional tale, or a biographical event. Use personification, similes, and metaphors in your imitation. It may be helpful to choose an emotional scene.)

The Ornamental Style

The *ornamental* style is adorned with metaphorical language and high-wrought imagery. The passage that follows is an example of such a style. This paragraph, taken from *A Tale of Two Cities,* is an extended metaphor, comparing the spilt red wine to blood. Through this metaphor, Dickens foreshadows the spilling of blood to come during his tale of the French Revolution. As the metaphorical wine flows through the streets, Dickens conveys the impact of this "wine" through the use of vivid, disturbing images and through the personification of the wine as it runs and "stains" everything and everyone in its path.

> The wine was red wine, and had stained the ground of the narrow street in the suburb of Saint Antoine, in Paris, where it was spilled. It had stained many hands, too, and many faces, and many naked feet, and many wooden shoes. The hands of the man who sawed the wood, left red marks on the billets; and the forehead of the woman who nursed her baby, was stained with the stain of the old rag she wound about her head again. Those who had been greedy with the staves of the cask, had acquired a tigerish smear about the mouth; and one tall joker so besmirched, his head more out of a long squalid bag of a nightcap than in it, scrawled upon a wall with his finger dipped in muddy wine-lees—*blood.*

—Charles Dickens, *A Tale of Two Cities*

> ➤ **EXERCISE 21.9: Style Practice**
> **Complete Steps** 1 and 2 (or Steps 1 and 3) of the writing options below. Advanced students will want to complete all steps. **Using the Checklist** located on page 183, correct your imitation. **Compare your writing** to the original passage. Were you able to imitate the style of the original passage? **Identify areas** in which your writing needs improvement. Identify areas in which you have bettered the original author.

Step 1: Read the model closely. Copy the model on the lines provided. By simply rewriting the model, you will become more intimately familiar with the style of the author.

Step 2: To further evaluate the author's style, write a brief outline to help you remember the content of the passage. When you are finished, put away the original model. Using your outline, rewrite the passage, maintaining the author's original style.

Step 3: Change the topic and create your own passage imitating the style of the original passage. (Suggested topic: Love of money is a sickness. The law is a weapon. Hatred is a heart of stone. Before you write, create a setting and characters to act out your metaphor. Another option is to read the poem by Emily Dickinson, which is located on page 186 in the Appendix, and rewrite it as prose, imitating the ornamental style of Charles Dickens.)

The Feeble Style

Feebleness in style consists in the use of an undue proportion of unimportant words, and of words not adapted to make much impression on the minds of readers. This style is useful when creating a character that is verbose, long-winded, and boring. The marriage proposal by Mr. Collins from Jane Austen's *Pride and Prejudice* provides us with just such an example.

"My reasons for marrying are, first, that I think it a right thing for every clergyman in easy circumstances (like myself) to set the example of matrimony in his parish; secondly, that I am convinced that it will add very greatly to my happiness; and thirdly—which perhaps I ought to have mentioned earlier, that it is the particular advice and recommendation of the very noble lady whom I have the honour of calling patroness. Twice has she condescended to give me her opinion (unasked too!) on this subject; and it was but the very Saturday night before I left Hunsford—between our pools at quadrille, while Mrs. Jenkinson was arranging Miss de Bourgh's footstool, that she said, 'Mr. Collins, you must marry. A clergyman like you must marry. Choose properly, choose a gentlewoman for *my* sake; and for your *own*, let her be an active, useful sort of person, not brought up high, but able to make a small income go a good way. This is my advice. Find such a woman as soon as you can, bring her to Hunsford, and I will visit her.' Allow me, by the way, to observe, my fair cousin, that I do not reckon the notice and kindness of Lady Catherine de Bourgh as among the least of the advantages in my power to offer. You will find her manners beyond anything I can describe; and your wit and vivacity, I think, must be acceptable to her, especially when tempered with the silence and respect which her rank will inevitably excite. Thus much for my general intention in favour of matrimony; it remains to be told why my views were directed towards Longbourn instead of my own neighbourhood, where I can assure you there are many amiable young women. But the fact is, that being, as I am, to inherit this estate after the death of your honoured father (who, however, may live many years longer), I could not satisfy myself without resolving to choose a wife from among his daughters, that the loss to them might be as little as possible, when the melancholy event takes place—which, however, as I have already said, may not be for several years. This has been my motive, my fair cousin, and I flatter myself it will not sink me in your esteem.

—Jane Austen, *Pride and Prejudice*

➤ **EXERCISE 21.10: Style Practice**
Complete Steps 1 and 2 (or Steps 1 and 3) of the writing options below. Advanced students will want to complete all steps. **Using the Checklist** located on page 183, correct your imitation. **Compare your writing** to the original passage. Were you able to imitate the style of the original passage? **Identify areas** in which your writing needs improvement. Identify areas in which you have bettered the original author.

Step 1: Read the model closely. Copy the model on the lines provided. By simply rewriting the model, you will become more intimately familiar with the style of the author.

Step 2: To further evaluate the author's style, write a brief outline to help you remember the content of the passage. When you are finished, put away the original model. Using your outline, rewrite the passage, maintaining the author's original style.

Step 3: Change the topic and create your own passage imitating the style of the original passage. (Suggestion: To brainstorm your new topic, complete the sentence: My reasons for _____ are . . .)

_____

_____

_____

_____

_____

_____

_____

_____

_____

_____

_____

_____

_____

_____

_____

_____

The Loose Style

The *loose* passage presents with long, languishing sentences. In the following example, these sentences are composed with clauses arranged in such a manner that the parenthetical expressions cause the sentences to mimic the soothing, unhurried ride that the characters are experiencing.

> Rena felt immensely relieved when the hour arrived at which she could take her departure, which was to be the signal for the breaking-up of the ball. She was driven home in Tryon's carriage, her brother accompanying them. The night was warm, and the drive homeward under the starlight, in the open carriage, had a soothing effect upon Rena's excited nerves. The calm restfulness of the night, the cool blue depths of the unclouded sky, the solemn croaking of the frogs in a distant swamp, were much more in harmony with her nature than the crowded brilliancy of the ball-room. She closed her eyes, and, leaning back in the carriage, thought of her mother, who she wished might have seen her daughter this night. A momentary pang of homesickness pierced her tender heart, and she furtively wiped away the tears that came into her eyes.
>
> —Charles Chesnutt, *The House Behind the Cedars*

➢ **EXERCISE 21.11: Style Practice**
Complete Steps 1 and 2 (or Steps 1 and 3) of the writing options below. Advanced students will want to complete all steps. **Using the Checklist** located on page 183, correct your imitation. **Compare your writing** to the original passage. Were you able to imitate the style of the original passage? **Identify areas** in which your writing needs improvement. Identify areas in which you have bettered the original author.

Step 1: Read the model closely. Copy the model on the lines provided. By simply rewriting the model, you will become more intimately familiar with the style of the author.

Step 2: To further evaluate the author's style, write a brief outline to help you remember the content of the passage. When you are finished, put away the original model. Using your outline, rewrite the passage, maintaining the author's original style.

Step 3: Change the topic and create your own passage imitating the style of the original passage. (Suggested topic: Describe a fun evening, a ride in a boat, a leisurely stroll in beautiful setting.)

Advanced Option: Read the introduction and satirical passage on page 187. Swift's purpose in writing this essay was to highlight the horrible treatment of the poor in Ireland. To imitate the loose style with satire, think of a serious topic, agree with the opposing opinion, use extreme hyperbolic language (such as eating children) and write with loose sentences.

The Plain Style

The *plain* style is a simple, easy, artless, and flowing style, easily written, and easily understood.

> By the side of a wood, in a country a long way off, ran a fine stream of water; and upon the stream there stood a mill. The miller's house was close by, and the miller, you must know, had a very beautiful daughter. She was, moreover, very shrewd and clever; and the miller was so proud of her, that he one day told the king of the land, who used to come and hunt in the wood, that his daughter could spin gold out of straw. Now this king was very fond of money; and when he heard the miller's boast his greediness was raised, and he sent for the girl to be brought before him. Then he led her to a chamber in his palace where there was a great heap of straw, and gave her a spinning-wheel, and said, 'All this must be spun into gold before morning, as you love your life.' It was in vain that the poor maiden said that it was only a silly boast of her father, for that she could do no such thing as spin straw into gold. The chamber door was locked, and she was left alone.
>
> —The Brothers Grimm, "Rumpelstiltskin"

> ➢ **EXERCISE 21.12: Style Practice**
> **Complete Steps** 1 and 2 (or Steps 1 and 3) of the writing options below. Advanced students will want to complete all steps. **Using the Checklist** located on page 183, correct your imitation. **Compare your writing** to the original passage. Were you able to imitate the style of the original passage? **Identify areas** in which your writing needs improvement. Identify areas in which you have bettered the original author.

Step 1: Read the model closely. Copy the model on the lines provided. By simply rewriting the model, you will become more intimately familiar with the style of the author.

Step 2: To further evaluate the author's style, write a brief outline to help you remember the content of the passage. When you are finished, put away the original model. Using your outline, rewrite the passage, maintaining the author's original style.

Step 3: Change the topic and create your own passage imitating the style of the original passage. (Suggested topics: Rewrite a well-known fairy tale using a different setting or different characters. You may also create an entirely new fairy tale.)

> **EXERCISE 21.13: Style Practice**
> Use the following idea.

      The man killed the dragon.

Rewrite the above sentence according to the style indicated. Refer to the style examples in the previous exercises. (Answers will vary.)

1. Forcible Style

_____

_____

_____

2. Vehement Style

_____

_____

_____

3. Elegant Style

_____

_____

_____

4. Brief Style

_____

_____

_____

5. Precise Style

_____

_____

_____

6. Copious Style

_____

_____

_____

7. Diffuse Style

_____

_____

_____

8. Neat Style

_____

_____

_____

9. Ornamental Style

_____

_____

_____

10. Feeble Style

_____

_____

_____

11. Loose Style

_____

_____

_____

12. Plain Style

_____

_____

_____

➤ **EXERCISE 21.14: Style Practice**
Use the following idea.

The petals floated on the wind.

Rewrite the above sentence according to the style indicated. Refer to the style examples in the previous exercises. (Answers will vary.)

1. Forcible Style

_____

_____

_____

2. Vehement Style

_____

_____

_____

3. Elegant Style

_____

_____

_____

4. Brief Style

_____

_____

_____

5. Precise Style

_____

_____

_____

6. Copious Style

_____

_____

_____

7. Diffuse Style

_____

_____

_____

8. Neat Style

_____

_____

_____

9. Ornamental Style

_____

_____

_____

10. Feeble Style

_____

_____

_____

11. Loose Style

_____

_____

_____

12. Plain Style

_____

_____

_____

> **EXERCISE 21.15: Style Practice**
Use the following idea.

The little girl tumbled down the hill.

Rewrite the above sentence according to the style indicated. Refer to the style examples in the previous exercises. (Answers will vary.)

1. Forcible Style

_____

_____

_____

2. Vehement Style

_____

_____

_____

3. Elegant Style

_____

_____

_____

4. Brief Style

_____

_____

_____

5. Precise Style

_____

_____

_____

6. Copious Style

_____

_____

_____

7. Diffuse Style

_____

_____

_____

8. Neat Style

_____

_____

_____

9. Ornamental Style

_____

_____

_____

10. Feeble Style

_____

_____

_____

11. Loose Style

_____

_____

_____

12. Plain Style

_____

_____

_____

22. Writing Dialogue with Style

Most modern literature includes an abundance of dialogue. For this reason, students should become intimately familiar with the appropriate use of dialogue.

General Rules for Writing Dialogue

Conversation brightens some fiction and ruins other. For that reason, it is important that students grasp a few rules when writing dialogue.

1. **Dialogue should be natural**. The speech of a character must be natural. It must reflect the dialogue of real people with whom we are familiar. It must be possible, logical and convincing.

2. **Dialogue should tell the story itself.** Unless it adds to the story, it should be omitted. A speech that tells nothing, that suggests nothing, that is dropped in simply as a "brightener," is a severe drag. Each sentence of speech must accomplish a definite end.

3. **Dialogue must portray character**. In the beginner's story, it is customary to make all the people talk alike; however, a person's speech defines him or her. A character's speech should clearly reveal the heart and soul of the speaker.

4. **Avoid an overuse of adverbs.** Only use adverbs when there is a definite verb that needs modifying. Otherwise, *let the verb speak for itself.*

To practice writing with dialogue, read the story that follows. When finished, complete the accompanying writing exercises.

"KIND sir, be so good as to notice a poor, hungry man. I have not tasted food for three days. I have not a five-kopeck piece for a night's lodging. I swear by God! For five years I was a village schoolmaster and lost my post through the intrigues of the Zemstvo. I was the victim of false witness. I have been out of a place for a year now."

Skvortsov, a Petersburg lawyer, looked at the speaker's tattered dark blue overcoat, at his muddy, drunken eyes, at the red patches on his cheeks, and it seemed to him that he had seen the man before.

"And now I am offered a post in the Kaluga province," the beggar continued, "but I have not the means for the journey there. Graciously help me! I am ashamed to ask, but . . . I am compelled by circumstances."

Skvortsov looked at his goloshes, of which one was shallow like a shoe, while the other came high up the leg like a boot, and suddenly remembered.

"Listen, the day before yesterday I met you in Sadovoy Street," he said, "and then you told me, not that you were a village schoolmaster, but that you were a student who had been expelled. Do you remember?"

"N-o. No, that cannot be so!" the beggar muttered in confusion. "I am a village schoolmaster, and if you wish it I can show you documents to prove it."

"That's enough lies! You called yourself a student, and even told me what you were expelled for. Do you remember?"

Skvortsov flushed, and with a look of disgust on his face turned away from the ragged figure.

"It's contemptible, sir!" he cried angrily. "It's a swindle! I'll hand you over to the police, curse you! You are poor and hungry, but that does not give you the right to lie so shamelessly!"

The ragged figure took hold of the door-handle and, like a bird in a snare, looked round the hall desperately.

"I . . . I am not lying," he muttered. "I can show documents."

"Who can believe you?" Skvortsov went on, still indignant. "To exploit the sympathy of the public for village schoolmasters and students—it's so low, so mean, so dirty! It's revolting!"

Skvortsov flew into a rage and gave the beggar a merciless scolding. The ragged fellow's insolent lying aroused his disgust and aversion, was an offence against what he, Skvortsov, loved and prized in himself: kindliness, a feeling heart, sympathy for the unhappy. By his lying, by his treacherous assault upon compassion, the individual had, as it were, defiled the charity which he liked to give to the poor with no misgivings in his heart. The beggar at first defended himself, protested with oaths, then he sank into silence and hung his head, overcome with shame.

"Sir!" he said, laying his hand on his heart, "I really was . . . lying! I am not a student and not a village schoolmaster. All that's mere invention! I used to be in the Russian choir, and I was turned out of it for drunkenness. But what can I do? Believe me, in God's name, I can't get on without lying—when I tell the truth no one will give me anything. With the truth one may die of hunger and freeze without a night's lodging! What you say is true, I understand that, but . . . what am I to do?"

"What are you to do? You ask what are you to do?" cried Skvortsov, going close up to him. "Work—that's what you must do! You must work!"

"Work. . . . I know that myself, but where can I get work?"

"Nonsense. You are young, strong, and healthy, and could always find work if you wanted to. But you know you are lazy, pampered, drunken! You reek of vodka like a pothouse! You have become false and corrupt to the marrow of your bones and fit for nothing but begging and lying! If you do graciously condescend to take work, you must have a job in an office, in the Russian choir, or as a billiard-marker, where you will have a salary and have nothing to do! But how would you like to undertake manual labour? I'll be bound, you wouldn't be a house porter or a factory hand! You are too genteel for that!"

"What things you say, really . . ." said the beggar, and he gave a bitter smile. "How can I get manual work? It's rather late for me to be a shopman, for in trade one has to begin from a boy; no one would take me as a house porter because I am not of that class . . . . And I could not get work in a factory; one must know a trade, and I know nothing."

"Nonsense! You always find some justification! Wouldn't you like to chop wood?"

"I would not refuse to, but the regular woodchoppers are out of work now."

"Oh, all idlers argue like that! As soon as you are offered anything you refuse it. Would you care to chop wood for me?"

"Certainly I will. . ."

"Very good, we shall see . . . Excellent. We'll see!" Skvortsov, in nervous haste; and not without malignant pleasure, rubbing his hands, summoned his cook from the kitchen.

"Here, Olga," he said to her, "take this gentleman to the shed and let him chop some wood."

The beggar shrugged his shoulders as though puzzled, and irresolutely followed the cook. It was evident from his demeanour that he had consented to go and chop wood, not because he was hungry and wanted to earn money, but simply from shame and *amour propre* because he had been taken at his word. It was clear, too, that he was suffering from the effects of vodka, that he was unwell, and felt not the faintest inclination to work.

Skvortsov hurried into the dining-room. There from the window which looked out into the yard he could see the woodshed and everything that happened in the yard. Standing at the window, Skvortsov saw the cook and the beggar come by the back way into the yard and go through the muddy snow to the woodshed. Olga scrutinized her companion angrily, and jerking her elbow unlocked the woodshed and angrily banged the door open.

"Most likely we interrupted the woman drinking her coffee," thought Skvortsov. "What a cross creature she is!"

Then he saw the pseudo-schoolmaster and pseudo-student seat himself on a block of wood, and, leaning his red cheeks upon his fists, sink into thought. The cook flung an axe at his feet, spat angrily on the ground, and, judging by the expression of her lips, began abusing him. The beggar drew a log of wood towards him irresolutely, set it up between his feet, and diffidently drew the axe across it. The log toppled and fell over. The beggar drew it towards him, breathed on his frozen hands, and again drew the axe along it as cautiously as though he were afraid of its hitting his golosh or chopping off his fingers. The log fell over again.

Skvortsov's wrath had passed off by now, he felt sore and ashamed at the thought that he had forced a pampered, drunken, and perhaps sick man to do hard, rough work in the cold.

"Never mind, let him go on . . ." he thought, going from the dining-room into his study. "I am doing it for his good!"

An hour later Olga appeared and announced that the wood had been chopped up.

"Here, give him half a rouble," said Skvortsov. "If he likes, let him come and chop wood on the first of every month. . . . There will always be work for him."

On the first of the month the beggar turned up and again earned half a rouble, though he could hardly stand. From that time forward he took to turning up frequently, and work was always found for him: sometimes he would sweep the snow into heaps, or clear up the shed, at another he used to beat the rugs and the mattresses. He always received thirty to forty kopecks for his work, and on one occasion an old pair of trousers was sent out to him.

When he moved, Skvortsov engaged him to assist in packing and moving the furniture. On this occasion the beggar was sober, gloomy, and silent; he scarcely touched the furniture, walked with hanging head behind the furniture vans, and did not even try to appear busy; he merely shivered with the cold, and was overcome with confusion when the men with the vans laughed at his idleness, feebleness, and ragged coat that had once been a gentleman's. After the removal Skvortsov sent for him.

"Well, I see my words have had an effect upon you," he said, giving him a rouble. "This is for your work. I see that you are sober and not disinclined to work. What is your name?"

"Lushkov."

"I can offer you better work, not so rough, Lushkov. Can you write?"

"Yes, sir."

"Then go with this note to-morrow to my colleague and he will give you some copying to do. Work, don't drink, and don't forget what I said to you. Good-bye."

Skvortsov, pleased that he had put a man in the path of rectitude, patted Lushkov genially on the shoulder, and even shook hands with him at parting.

Lushkov took the letter, departed, and from that time forward did not come to the back-yard for work.

Two years passed. One day as Skvortsov was standing at the ticket-office of a theatre, paying for his ticket, he saw beside him a little man with a lambskin collar and a shabby cat's-skin cap. The man timidly asked the clerk for a gallery ticket and paid for it with kopecks.

"Lushkov, is it you?" asked Skvortsov, recognizing in the little man his former woodchopper. "Well, what are you doing? Are you getting on all right?"

"Pretty well. . . . I am in a notary's office now. I earn thirty-five roubles."

"Well, thank God, that's capital. I rejoice for you. I am very, very glad, Lushkov. You know, in a way, you are my godson. It was I who shoved you into the right way. Do you remember what a scolding I gave you, eh? You almost sank through the floor that time. Well, thank you, my dear fellow, for remembering my words."

"Thank you too," said Lushkov. "If I had not come to you that day, maybe I should be calling myself a schoolmaster or a student still. Yes, in your house I was saved, and climbed out of the pit."

"I am very, very glad."

"Thank you for your kind words and deeds. What you said that day was excellent. I am grateful to you and to your cook, God bless that kind, noble-hearted woman. What you said that day was excellent; I am indebted to you as long as I live, of course, but it was your cook, Olga, who really saved me."

"How was that?"

"Why, it was like this. I used to come to you to chop wood and she would begin: 'Ah, you drunkard! You God-forsaken man! And yet death does not take you!' and then she would sit opposite me, lamenting, looking into my face and wailing: 'You unlucky fellow! You have no gladness in this world, and in the next you will burn in hell, poor drunkard! You poor sorrowful creature!' and she always went on in that style, you know. How often she upset herself, and how many tears she shed over me I can't tell you. But what affected me most—she chopped the wood for me! Do you know, sir, I never chopped a single log for you—she did it all! How it was she saved me, how it was I changed, looking at her, and gave up drinking, I can't explain. I only know that what she said and the noble way she behaved brought about a change in my soul, and I shall never forget it. It's time to go up, though, they are just going to ring the bell."

Lushkov bowed and went off to the gallery.

—Anton Chekov "The Beggar"

➤ **EXERCISE 22.1: Writing Dialogue with Style**
The following exercise is designed around the plain style. As you complete the exercises, write your dialogue in a simple, easily written, and easily understood manner. Complete one (or more) of the steps listed on the following page. Advanced students will want to complete all five steps. See page 31 for a review of dialogue punctuation.

Step 1: Copy the bolded paragraphs on the lines provided. By simply rewriting the model, you will become more intimately familiar with the art of writing dialoguing.

Step 2: Rewrite the penultimate paragraph that begins with the sentence, "Why, it was like this." Write in dialogue the words of the cook as she lambasts and serves the poor drunkard all at the same time. Your paragraph should not be a rewrite of the repeated words mentioned by Lushkov, but rather an expansion of the interaction and wordplay between Lushkov and Olga the cook. Be creative.

Step 3: Rewrite the above story, using a modern setting and modern characters. Use appropriate dialogue for the new characters.

Step 4: As you can see, most of this short story is written in dialogue. The dialogue itself tells the story. Following the example selection, write a short story written predominantly in dialogue. Be sure to use the necessary explanatory modifiers and make each character's voice distinct.

Step 5: Using the Checklist located on page 183, correct your imitation.

23. Shifting Style at Will

"Success in writing is not the result of a flash of genius but of study and practice."

—William Kane

The exercises in this chapter challenge students to transform passages from one style to another. The result will sometimes produce passages that are greatly improved. Other times the resulting passages will fall somewhere between awkward and ludicrous.

The goal of these final exercises is that students acquire greater writing flexibility. This flexibility will enable students to gain greater skill at producing the literary effects they desire. In any single well-written novel, it is common to find several writing styles. Authors modify their writing styles to suit the varying personalities of the characters they create.

It is also important that novice writers acquire greater facility in their ability to choose the appropriate style for the topic and purpose of each writing endeavor. The ultimate goal of all writing is communication, and in order to effectively communicate, writers must understand that their audience, their topic, and their purpose dictate the style with which they write any particular composition.

Note: Some of these passages demonstrate a strong command of the language with their high-level word choices. As you transform the style of the passage, be sure to choose vocabulary that is more appropriate for the new style and meets your level of English. Use a thesaurus if needed.

> **EXERCISE 23.1: Shifting Style**
> The following passage is written in a forceful style. On the following page, rewrite the passage so that it is written in a loose style. Refer to the example given on page 143.

The graces taught in the schools, the costly ornaments, and studied contrivances of speech, shock and disgust men, when their own lives, and the fate of their wives, their children, and their country, hang on the decision of the hour. Then words have lost their power, rhetoric is vain, and all elaborate oratory is contemptible. Even genius itself then feels rebuked, and subdued, as in the presence of higher qualities. Then, patriotism is eloquent; then, self-devotion is eloquent. The clear conception, outrunning the deductions of logic, the high purpose, the firm resolve, the dauntless spirit, speaking on the tongue, beaming from the eye, informing every feature, and urging the whole man onward, right onward to his object,—this, this is eloquence; or rather it is something greater and higher than all eloquence, it is action, noble, sublime, godlike action.

—Webster

> **EXERCISE 23.2: Shifting Style**
The following passage is written in an easy style. On the lines that follow, rewrite the passage so that it is written in a vehement style. Refer to the example given on page 113.

The young of all animals appear to receive pleasure simply from the exercise of their limbs and bodily faculties, without reference to any end to be attained, or any use to be answered by the exertion. A child, without knowing any thing of the use of language, is in a high degree delighted with being able to speak. Its incessant repetition of a few articulate sounds, or, perhaps, of a single word, which it has learned to pronounce, proves this point clearly. Nor is it less pleased with its first successful endeavours to walk, or rather, to run, (which precedes walking), although entirely ignorant of the importance of the attainment to its future life, and even without applying it to any present purpose. A child is delighted with speaking, without having anything to say and with walking, without knowing whither to go. And, previously to both these, it is reasonable to believe, that the waking hours of infancy are agreeably taken up with the exercise of vision, or, perhaps, more properly speaking, with learning to see.

—Paley, "Natural Theology"

➤ EXERCISE 23.3: Shifting Style

The following passage is written in an ornamental style. On the lines that follow, rewrite the passage so that it is written in a brief style. Refer to the example given on page 119.

It is not in man's power to alter the course of the sun; but it is often in his power to cause the sun to shine or not to shine upon him; if he withdraws from his beams, or spreads a curtain before him, the sun no longer shines upon him; if he quits the shade, or removes the curtain, the light is restored to him; and though no change is in the meantime effected in the heavenly luminary, but only in himself, the result is the same as if it were. Nor is the immutability of God any reason why the returning sinner, who tears away the veil of prejudice or of indifference, should not again be blessed with the sunshine of Divine favor.

—Whatley, *Elements of Rhetoric*

> **EXERCISE 23.4: Shifting Style**
> The following passage is written in a brief style. On the lines that follow, rewrite the passage so that it is written in a feeble style. Refer to the example given on page 137.

You have still an honorable part to act. The affections of your subjects may still be recovered. But, before you subdue their hearts, you must gain a noble victory over your own. Discard those little personal resentments, which have too long directed your public conduct.

Without consulting your minister, call together your whole council. Let it appear to the public, that you can determine and act for yourself. Come forward to your people. Lay aside the wretched formalities of a king, and speak to your subjects with the spirit of a man, and in the language of a gentleman. Tell them you have been fatally deceived. The acknowledgment will be no disgrace, but rather an honor, to your understanding. Tell them you are determined to remove every cause of complaint against your government; that you will give your confidence to no man, who does not possess the confidence of your subjects. They will then do justice to their representatives and to themselves.

—Junius, *Letters of Junius*

The following passage is written in a diffuse style. On the lines that follow, rewrite the passage so that it is written in a plain style. Refer to the example given on page 146.

Happy that man, who, unembarrassed by vulgar cares, master of himself, his time, and fortune, spends his time in making himself wiser, and his fortune in making others (and therefore himself) happier: who, as the will and understanding are the two ennobling faculties of the soul, thinks himself not complete, till his understanding be beautified with the valuable furniture of knowledge, as well as his will enriched with every virtue; who has furnished himself with all the advantages to relish solitude, and enliven conversation; when serious, not sullen; and when cheerful, not indiscreetly gay; his ambition, not to be admired for a false glare of greatness, but to be beloved for the gentle and sober lustre of his wisdom and goodness. The greatest minister of state has not more business to do in a public capacity, than he, and indeed every man else, may find in the retired and still scenes of life. Even in his private walks, every thing that is visible convinceth him there is present a Being invisible. Aided by natural philosophy, he reads plain, legible traces of the Divinity in every thing he meets: he sees the Deity in every tree, as well as Moses did in the burning bush, though not in so glaring a manner: and when he sees him, he adores him with the tribute of a grateful heart.

—Seed, *Discourses on Several Important Subjects*

> **EXERCISE 23.6: Shifting Style**
The following passage is written in a vehement style. On the lines that follow, rewrite the passage so that it is written in an ornamental style. Refer to the example given on page 136.

You speak like a boy,—like a boy, who thinks the old, gnarled oak can be twisted as easily as the young sapling. Can I forget that I have been branded as an outlaw, stigmatized as a traitor, a price set on my head as if I had been a wolf, my family treated as the dam and cubs of the hill-fox, whom all may torment, vilify, degrade, and insult;—the very name which came to me from a long and noble line of martial ancestors, denounced, as if it were a spell to conjure up the devil with?

And they shall find that the name they have dared to proscribe,—that the name of MacGregor *is* a spell to raise the wild devil withal. *They* shall hear of my vengeance, that would scorn to listen to the story of my wrongs. The miserable Highland drover, bankrupt, barefooted, stripped of all, dishonored and hunted down, because the avarice of others grasped at more than that poor all could pay, shall burst on them in an awful change. They that scoffed at the grovelling worm, and trod upon him, may cry and howl when they see the stoop of the flying and fiery-mouthed dragon.

—Sir Walter Scott, *The Waverly Novels*

_____

_____

_____

_____

_____

_____

_____

_____

_____

_____

_____

_____

_____

_____

_____

The following passage is written in a copious style. On the lines that follow, rewrite the passage so that it is written in a precise style. Refer to the example given on page 122.

In order to discern where man's true honor lies, we must look, not to any adventitious circumstances of fortune; not to any single sparkling quality; but to the whole of what forms a man; what entitles him, as such, to rank high among that class of beings to which he belongs; in a word, we must look to the mind and the soul. A mind superior to fear, to selfish interest and corruption; a mind governed by the principles of uniform rectitude and integrity; the same in prosperity and adversity; which no bribe can seduce, nor terror overawe; neither by pleasure melted into effeminacy, nor by distress sunk into dejection: such is the mind which forms the distinction and eminence of man. One, who in no situation of life, is either ashamed or afraid of discharging his duty, and acting his proper part with firmness and constancy; true to the God whom he worships, and true to the faith in which he professes to believe: full of affection to his brethren of mankind; faithful to his friends, generous to his enemies, warm with compassion to the unfortunate; self-denying to little private interests and pleasures, but zealous for public interest and happiness: magnanimous, without being proud; humble, without being mean; just, without being harsh; simple in his manners, but manly in his feelings; on whose words we can entirely rely; whose countenance never deceives us; whose professions of kindness are the effusions of his heart; one, in fine, whom, independent of any views of advantage, we would choose for a superior, could trust in as a friend, and could love as a brother,—this is the man, whom in our heart, above all others, we do, we must honor.

—Dr. Blair, "The True Honor of Man"

_____

_____

_____

_____

_____

_____

_____

_____

_____

_____

➤ **EXERCISE 23.8: Shifting Style**

The following passage is written in an ornamental style. On the lines that follow, rewrite the passage so that it is written in a neat style. Refer to the example given on page 132.

Beautiful Night! with thy balm and softness, and thy maternal love spreading over this troubled earth with a deep and still sanctity,—and you, fresh-breathing winds, and fragrant herbs and grass, and matted trees, which the sun never pierces, and where a vague spirit moving calls, as a tribute, tenderness from meditation, and poetry from thought,—forgive me, for I have wronged you. It is from you that the dead speak, and their whispered and sweet voices have tidings of consolation and joy,—it is you, and the murmur of the waters, and the humming stillness of noon, and the melodious stars, which have tones for the heart, not ear, and whatever in the living lyres of the universe have harmony and intelligence,—it is you, all of you, that are the organs of a love which has only escaped from clay to blend itself with the great elements, and become with them, creating and universal! O beautiful and soothing mystery of nature, that while the spirit quits the earth, the robes which on earth it wore remain to hallow this world to the survivors! remain not only to moulder and decay, but to revive, to remingle with the life around, and to give, even in the imperishability of matter, a type of the immortal essence of the soul!

—Bulwer, *The Southern Review, Volume 3*

_____

_____

_____

_____

_____

_____

_____

_____

_____

_____

_____

_____

_____

> **EXERCISE 23.9: Shifting Style**
The following passage is written in an elegant style. On the lines that follow, rewrite the passage so that it is written in a diffuse style. Refer to the example given on page 128.

Right conceptions of the glory of our ancestors are alone to be attained by analyzing their virtues. These virtues, indeed, are not seen charactered in breathing bronze, or in living marble. Our ancestors have left no Corinthian temples on our hills, no Gothic cathedrals on our plains, no proud pyramid, no storied obelisk in our cities. But mind is there. Sagacious enterprise is there. An active, vigorous, intelligent, moral population throng our cities, and predominate in our fields; men, patient of labor, submissive to law, respectful to authority, regardful of right, faithful to liberty. These are the monuments of our ancestors. They stand immutable and immortal, in the social, moral, and intellectual condition of their descendants. They exist in the spirit, which their precepts instilled, and their example implanted.

—Josiah Quincy, "An Address to the Citizens of Boston"

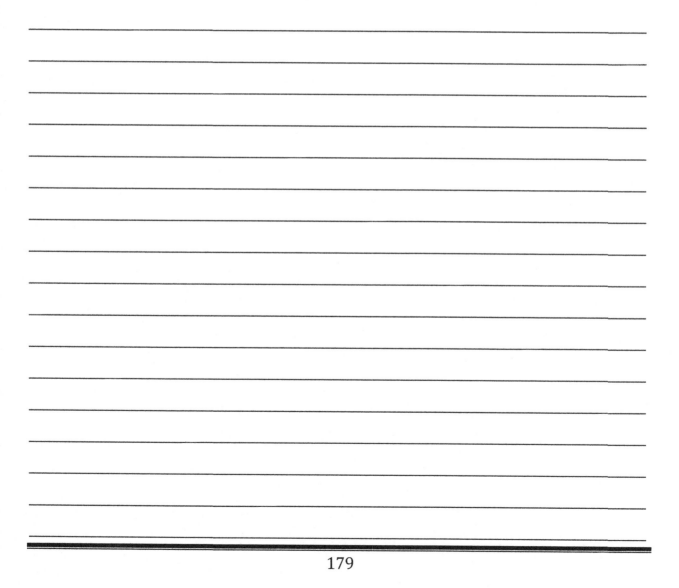

Appendices

Appendix A: The Elements of Style Checklist

✓	**I.**	**Elementary Rules of Usage**
	1.	Check your possessive nouns.
		a. Are singular possessives formed with 's?
		b. Are plural possessives formed with s'?
	2.	Check your series lists (3 or more items).
		a. Is there a comma between each item in the series?
	3.	Check your parenthetic expressions.
		a. Are there commas on **both** sides of the expression (nonrestrictive clause)?
		b. Are there **no commas** marking restrictive clauses?
	4.	Check your sentence structure.
		a. Are independent clauses in a sentence separated by a comma and coordinating conjunction (and, but, or, for, nor, so, yet)?
		b. Is there a comma after dependent clauses that begin sentences?
		c. Are dominant ideas marked through the use of subordinate clauses?
	5.	Check your independent clauses in the same sentence.
		a. Are they separated by a semicolon or comma plus coordinating conjunction?
	6.	Check your dependent clauses and phrases.
		a. Are they connected to an independent clause?
		b. (Are there fragments?)
	7.	Check your phrases at the beginning of sentences.
		a. Do the pre-subject phrases refer to the grammatical subject of the sentence?
✓	**II.**	**Elementary Composition**
	8.	Check your sentence lengths.
		a. Are they varied, with some long and some short sentences?
	9.	Check your paragraph content.
		a. Does each paragraph have one and only one topic?
		b. If you have dialogue,
		i. Is each character's utterance a new paragraph?
		ii. Is all speech marked by beginning and ending quotation marks?
	10.	Check your paragraph structure.
		a. Does each paragraph have a topic sentence?
		b. Does each paragraph have a concluding sentence that summarizes the point of the paragraph?
		c. Are all sentences in the paragraph well-organized, with all relevant information on each point presented together?
		d. Does each paragraph have narrative devices (transitions) between ideas within the paragraph?
		e. If the composition is longer than one paragraph, does each paragraph after the first contain a transition?

		11. Consider your purpose.
		a. If a narrative, are the events related chronologically?
		b. If a description, is it descriptive enough to create a clear image in the reader's mind?
		c. If an exposition, is it well explained?
		i. If paraphrasing, did you choose different words and structures from the original?
		12. Check passive voice.
		a. Identify the passive voice sentences in your work. Do they need to be in passive voice?
		b. Change passive to active whenever possible and reasonable.
		13. Check negative statements.
		a. Have you used *not*?
		b. Can you replace instances of *not*?
		14. Check language choices.
		a. Is your language definite, specific and concrete?
		15. Consider the words you've used.
		a. Are there excess words you can eliminate?
		16. Check your loose sentences.
		a. Make sure you don't have too many compound sentences (those using a coordinating conjunction) in a row.
		b. Vary your loose sentences with periodic sentences when possible.
		17. Check your parallel structure.
		a. Do all items in a list or intended to be contrasted against each other have the same base structure?
		18. Check your word order.
		a. Are the modifiers right next to the nouns they modify?
		19. Check your tense.
		a. Is it consistent throughout the writing?
✓	**III.**	**Secrets of Style**
		20. Is your style appropriate for your topic, purpose, and audience? Consider the following styles.
		a. Forcible Style
		b. Vehement Style
		c. Elegant Style
		d. Brief Style
		e. Precise Style
		f. Copious Style
		g. Diffuse Style
		h. Neat Style
		i. Ornamental Style
		j. Feeble Style
		k. Loose Style
		l. Plain Style

Benjamin Franklin's 13 Virtues

from Benjamin Franklin's Autobiography

In the various enumerations of the moral virtues I had met with in my reading, I found the catalogue more or less numerous, as different writers included more or fewer ideas under the same name. Temperance, for example, was by some confined to eating and drinking, while by others it was extended to mean the moderating of every other pleasure, appetite, inclination, or passion, bodily or mental, even to our avarice and ambition. I proposed to myself, for the sake of clearness, to use rather more names, with fewer ideas annexed to each, than a few names with more ideas; and I included under thirteen names of virtues all that at that time occurred to me as necessary or desirable, and annexed to each a short precept, which fully expressed the extent I gave to its meaning. These names of virtues, with their precepts, were:

TEMPERANCE.	Eat not to dullness; drink not to elevation.
SILENCE.	Speak not but what may benefit others or yourself; avoid trifling conversation.
ORDER.	Let all your things have their places; let each part of your business have its time.
RESOLUTION.	Resolve to perform what you ought; perform without fail what you resolve.
FRUGALITY.	Make no expense but to do good to others or yourself; i.e., waste nothing.
INDUSTRY.	Lose no time; be always employed in something useful; cut off all unnecessary actions.
SINCERITY.	Use no hurtful deceit; think innocently and justly, and if you speak, speak accordingly.
JUSTICE.	Wrong none by doing injuries, or omitting the benefits that are your duty.
MODERATION.	Avoid extremes; forbear resenting injuries so much as you think they deserve.
CLEANLINESS.	Tolerate no uncleanliness in body, cloths, or habitation.
TRANQUILLITY.	Be not disturbed at trifles, or at accidents common or unavoidable.
CHASTITY.	Rarely use venery but for health or offspring, never to dullness, weakness, or the injury of your own or another's peace or reputation.
HUMILITY.	Imitate Jesus and Socrates.

Hope is the Thing with Feathers

The following poem by Emily Dickinson is an extended metaphor.

> Hope is the thing with feathers
> That perches in the soul,
> And sings the tune without the words,
> And never stops at all,
>
> And sweetest in the gale is heard;
> And sore must be the storm
> That could abash the little bird
> That kept so many warm.
>
> I've heard it in the chilliest land,
> And on the strangest sea;
> Yet, never, in extremity,
> It asked a crumb of me.

Appendix D: Supporting Material for Exercise 21.11.

A Modest Proposal

For Preventing the Children of Poor People in Ireland from Being a Burden to Their Parents or Country, and for Making Them Beneficial to the Public. 1729

THE following satirical essay remains as the chief monument to the wrongs of Ireland during Swift's lifetime. We need not attempt, as Swift and others did, to assign the blame for these wrongs to any one party. The fates had fought against the country: the dregs of every controversy that had disturbed England had been thrown upon her, and besides all the mischances bred of her own history, she had suffered from the feuds that had spent themselves in England, and had dragged on the bitter remnants of their venom in Ireland. That the miseries which form the text of Swift's essay are not exaggerated by him may be proved from the bare statistics and facts that are repeated in the letters and pamphlets of the day.

Swift's treatment of them has been censured as a heartless play of humor upon human misery. But so to read it, is indeed to mistake the whole meaning of Swift's sarcasm, when, as here, it is illumined by the white heat of indignation. Humor is what Swift is here thinking least about. He adopts, it is true, the phraseology, **the outward style,** the mannerisms of the humorist. But it is only in order to give intensity to the irony.

It is difficult to believe that any one, reading this essay without perverse bias, can fail to see how all feelings are mastered in its author, by the overpowering indignation at wrong, and sadness at the sight of hopeless misery. Swift's character did not, indeed, permit him to give free utterance to his compassion—perhaps even prevented compassion being his chief impulse. With him anger served the purpose better, and lent to his pen a force which compassion could not have given: but none the less did it, in his own words, ' tear his heart.'

We read this essay with admiration, indeed, for its consummate irony, but at the same time, *recognizing in it a deadly seriousness of purpose that pierces through every line of that irony.*
        —adapted from *Swift: Selections from His Works: Volume 2 by* Henry Craik

   It is a melancholy object to those, who walk through this great town, or travel in the country, when they see the streets, the roads and cabbin-doors crowded with beggars of the female sex, followed by three, four, or six children, all in rags, and importuning every passenger for an alms. These mothers instead of being able to work for their honest livelihood, are forced to employ all their time in stroling to beg sustenance for their helpless infants who, as they grow up, either turn thieves for want of work, or leave their dear native country, to fight for the Pretender in Spain, or sell themselves to the Barbadoes.

I think it is agreed by all parties, that this prodigious number of children in the arms, or on the backs, or at the heels of their mothers, and frequently of their fathers, is in the present deplorable state of the kingdom, a very great additional grievance; and therefore whoever could find out a fair, cheap and easy method of making these children sound and useful members of the common-wealth, would deserve so well of the publick, as to have his statue set up for a preserver of the nation.

But my intention is very far from being confined to provide only for the children of professed beggars: it is of a much greater extent, and shall take in the whole number of infants at a certain age, who are born of parents in effect as little able to support them, as those who demand our charity in the streets.

As to my own part, having turned my thoughts for many years, upon this important subject, and maturely weighed the several schemes of our projectors, I have always found them grossly mistaken in their computation. It is true, a child just dropt from its dam, may be supported by her milk, for a solar year, with little other nourishment: at most not above the value of two shillings, which the mother may certainly get, or the value in scraps, by her lawful occupation of begging; and it is exactly at one year old that I propose to provide for them in such a manner, as, instead of being a charge upon their parents, or the parish, or wanting food and raiment for the rest of their lives, they shall, on the contrary, contribute to the feeding, and partly to the cloathing of many thousands.

There is likewise another great advantage in my scheme, that it will prevent those voluntary abortions, and that horrid practice of women murdering their bastard children, alas! too frequent among us, sacrificing the poor innocent babes, I doubt, more to avoid the expence than the shame, which would move tears and pity in the most savage and inhuman breast.

The number of souls in this kingdom being usually reckoned one million and a half, of these I calculate there may be about two hundred thousand couple whose wives are breeders; from which number I subtract thirty thousand couple, who are able to maintain their own children, (although I apprehend there cannot be so many, under the present distresses of the kingdom) but this being granted, there will remain an hundred and seventy thousand breeders. I again subtract fifty thousand, for those women who miscarry, or whose children die by accident or disease within the year. There only remain an hundred and twenty thousand children of poor parents annually born. The question therefore is, How this number shall be reared, and provided for? which, as I have already said, under the present situation of affairs, is utterly impossible by all the methods hitherto proposed. For we can neither employ them in handicraft or agriculture; they neither build houses, (I mean in the country) nor cultivate land: they can very seldom pick up a livelihood by stealing till they arrive at six years old; except where they are of towardly parts, although I confess they learn the rudiments much earlier; during which time they can however be properly looked upon only as probationers: As I have been informed by a principal gentleman in the county of Cavan, who protested to me, that he never knew above one or two instances under the age of six, even in a part of the kingdom so renowned for the quickest proficiency in that art.

I am assured by our merchants, that a boy or a girl before twelve years old, is no saleable commodity, and even when they come to this age, they will not yield above three pounds, or three pounds and half a crown at most, on the exchange; which cannot turn to account either to the parents or kingdom, the charge of nutriments and rags having been at least four times that value.

I shall now therefore humbly propose my own thoughts, which I hope will not be liable to the least objection.

I have been assured by a very knowing American of my acquaintance in London, that a young healthy child well nursed, is, at a year old, a most delicious nourishing and wholesome food, whether stewed, roasted, baked, or boiled; and I make no doubt that it will equally serve in a fricasie, or a ragoust.

I do therefore humbly offer it to publick consideration, that of the hundred and twenty thousand children, already computed, twenty thousand may be reserved for breed, whereof only one fourth part to be males; which is more than we allow to sheep, black cattle, or swine, and my reason is, that these children are seldom the fruits of marriage, a circumstance not much regarded by our savages, therefore, one male will be sufficient to serve four females. That the remaining hundred thousand may, at a year old, be offered in sale to the persons of quality and fortune, through the kingdom, always advising the mother to let them suck plentifully in the last month, so as to render them plump, and fat for a good table. A child will make two dishes at an entertainment for friends, and when the family dines alone, the fore or hind quarter will make a reasonable dish, and seasoned with a little pepper or salt, will be very good boiled on the fourth day, especially in winter.

I have reckoned upon a medium, that a child just born will weigh 12 pounds, and in a solar year, if tolerably nursed, encreaseth to 28 pounds.

I grant this food will be somewhat dear, and therefore very proper for landlords, who, as they have already devoured most of the parents, seem to have the best title to the children.

Example Answers 1.1: Answers will vary.

1. The boys' room is always a mess.
2. They often have readings at the children's library.
3. Charles's friend is named Bill.
4. The team's mascot is a cougar.
5. Her hair's color is a beautiful red.
6. It's sad to see the once-cherished doll abandoned with its hair matted and its eyes plucked out.
7. Those chores are yours, and you're responsible for your chores.
8. Who's going to identify those who signed up for the conference and those whose contributions have already been received?

Answers 3.1: (1. ..., who slowly lifted his head,... 2. ..., which is pure carbon,... 3. ..., who my sister is dating,..., 4. No change, 5. No change, 6. No change, 7. No change, 8. , the first president of the U. S.)

Answers 3.3: (1. talk, 2. honest, 3. difficulties, 4. lasts, 5. heard, 6. country, 7. comes,)

Example Answers 4.1:

1. They are determined to have their own way, yet they know they will suffer for their willfulness.
Though they will suffer for their willfulness, they are determined to have their own way.
2. I cannot go to the circus, for I have no money.
I cannot go to the circus because I have no money.
3. No one gave him a ticket, so he cannot go to the circus.
Since no one gave him a ticket, he cannot go to the circus.
4. He walks slowly, for he is very tired.
He walks slowly when he is very tired.

Example Answers 6.1: Answers will vary.

1. It was amazing that we had taken him by surprise.
2. When we rose the next morning, having slept well, we were ready to take on the day.
3. Through no fault of his, he was shunned by his loved ones.
4. Though the whole experience left no pleasant memory, it was important to his personal growth.
5. To relieve his suffering somewhat, he took an aspirin.
6. If that is true and if the conditions are as favorable as you say, we should all see some epic waves in the surf tomorrow.
7. When Earth's last picture is painted, that will be the end of mankind's presence here.

Answers 7.1: Answers will vary.
1. While eating my dinner yesterday evening, I
2. Writing a very tedious essay, I
3. Peeping through our keyhole, I [or we]
4. Failing to wind my watch, I
5. Dropping my watch on the hardwood floor, I
6. Walking through the woods, John

Answers 9.1: Sentences that do not belong: This famous man is said to have invented stoves. One of Franklin's most celebrated writings is "Poor Richard's Almanac."

Note: These sentences violate the law of unity because they relate to Franklin's adult life, not his childhood.

Answer 9.2: Below is the original punctuation. When checking your work, remember there is often more than one correct way to punctuate dialogue.

"Come in!" said Holmes.

A man entered who could hardly have been less than six feet six inches in height, with the chest and limbs of a Hercules. His dress was rich with a richness which would, in England, be looked upon as akin to bad taste. Heavy bands of astrakhan were slashed across the sleeves and fronts of his double-breasted coat, while the deep blue cloak which was thrown over his shoulders was lined with flame-coloured silk and secured at the neck with a brooch which consisted of a single flaming beryl. Boots which extended halfway up his calves, and which were trimmed at the tops with rich brown fur, completed the impression of barbaric opulence which was suggested by his whole appearance. He carried a broad-brimmed hat in his hand, while he wore across the upper part of his face, extending down past the cheekbones, a black vizard mask, which he had apparently adjusted that very moment, for his hand was still raised to it as he entered. From the lower part of the face he appeared to be a man of strong character, with a thick, hanging lip, and a long, straight chin suggestive of resolution pushed to the length of obstinacy.

"You had my note?" he asked with a deep harsh voice and a strongly marked German accent. "I told you that I would call." He looked from one to the other of us, as if uncertain which to address.

"Pray take a seat," said Holmes. "This is my friend and colleague, Dr. Watson, who is occasionally good enough to help me in my cases. Whom have I the honour to address?"

"You may address me as the Count Von Kramm, a Bohemian nobleman. I understand that this gentleman, your friend, is a man of honour and discretion, whom I may trust with a matter of the most extreme importance. If not, I should much prefer to communicate with you alone."

I rose to go, but Holmes caught me by the wrist and pushed me back into my chair. "It is both, or none," said he. "You may say before this gentleman anything which you may say to me."

Answer 10.1: The proposition is peace.

In the previous paragraph, the writer's purpose is to explain and enforce the topic sentence. After reading the topic sentence, one is inclined to ask, "What kind of peace? How is it to be secured?" The second sentence proceeds to tell what kind of peace it is *not;* the third defines peace briefly; the fourth, a little more at length; and the last sentence explains more definitely the kind of peace proposed. Not until this last sentence, in fact, is the exact nature of this peace determined. In each of these last three sentences there is repetition of the same idea, but with a new twist added each time. The paragraph follows the principles perfectly and develops the idea presented in the topic sentence by means of *definition, repetition,* and *explanation.*

Answer 10.2: I seemed to see a rending and upheaving of all nature.

Example Answer 10.4:

Taro root is a starchy, nutrient-rich root vegetable. It's high in fiber and has a rich antioxidant content to help fight diseases of many kinds and improve vision. Loaded with potassium, it helps with circulation. Its high vitamin C levels boost the immune system and help combat immunodeficiency conditions. Rich also in iron and copper, taro reduces the chances of developing anemia and stimulates blood flow. It's also pretty high in calories, unfortunately. Because of its higher nutrient content compared with a potato, you can easily substitute it for potato in your recipes. Whatever you can do with a potato, you can do with taro. Its flavor and texture are more interesting than a potato's though. It makes an easy side dish, whether mashed, simmered, stewed, or fried. Taro is a surprisingly nutrient-rich alternative to the usual starchy vegetable options.

Example Answers 10.5: Answers will vary.

Like all other parts of your body, your teeth have to last you a lifetime. However, unlike other parts of your body, teeth don't heal themselves when they have been damaged. Once you damage a tooth, you have to get it professionally fixed. It will not heal on its own. Therefore, responsible oral care will help your teeth last long into your elder years.

One way to practice responsible oral care is with regular brushing. Brushing your teeth regularly helps ensure your teeth will last for many years. Brushing removes bacteria and other tiny matter that builds up on your teeth and causes problems such as cavities and periodontitis, or worse. It's important to brush carefully, ensuring you reach all surfaces of all teeth and scrub them as clean as you can with every brushing.

Another important, yet often overlooked, aspect of oral hygiene is flossing. Flossing your teeth every day is important. Dental floss reaches in between your teeth where your brush doesn't reach and cleans the gum area between your teeth as well as the sides of your teeth.

Daily practices determine the overall health of your teeth, but visiting a dentist regularly for a cleaning and examination helps ensure your teeth remain healthy. With their tiny equipment, dentists can see problem areas just beginning to form and guide you to best avoid them through targeted oral care.

Example Answers 12.1: **Answers will vary.**

1. People around the world heard the shot.
2. The mountain lion viciously attacked the boy.
3. Many people dream of living in an exotic paradise and sipping fresh coconut water every morning.
4. Her delightful command of satire and irony, in the proper company, led others to perceive her as intelligent and humorous.
5. The company gave them a second chance, but will not extend a third.
6. Smiling, their large group of friends had arrived to see Sal and Serena off on their journey.

Answers 13.1: ***Answers will vary.***

1. She forgot to pay her phone bill.
2. She ignored her college professor's recommendation that she review her calculus notes every day.
3. We need more research studies on environmental communication.
4. That response is inaccurate.
5. Please contact me if you need to.
6. We lack enough solid information to make a decision.
7. I remain unpersuaded that the cause is valid.
8. The reports are incomplete and we are unable to offer a valid assessment at this time.

Example Answers 14.1: ***Answers will vary.***

1. His home sat in the middle of the mountainside, engulfed in a rich, lush pine forest.
2. The tropical fruit papaya contains about 150 percent of the daily recommended intake of vitamin C, while its tropical neighbor soursop is a nutrient powerhouse with 17 percent of the daily recommended intake of potassium, 28 percent of fiber, 77 percent of vitamin C, 11 percent of magnesium, and 7 percent of iron in a single one-cup serving.
3. Strolling down the street, he noticed tidy Victorian homes lining both sides, punctuated with neatly trimmed cypress trees.
4. Observing the ways people use language differently in other cultures and the different ways people process and problem-solve helps her gain insight into humanity in general and gives her great reasons to travel.
5. In some countries, selling even a very small amount of marijuana is punishable by decapitation.
6. She is selfless, intelligent, and patient.
7. My home town sits in a valley among gently rolling hills.

Example Answers 15.1: Answers will vary.

1. He refused to go because he was stubborn.
2. The sentence that begins the paragraph is awkward.
3. Some penalties for rule-breaking are severe.
4. We planned our vacation for October because airfares tend to go down then.
5. Much knowledge remains unknown, but scientists continue to advance human understanding.

Answers 16.1: Answers will vary.

1. In the passageway behind the courthouse, she awaited her death.
2. Even though we were fairly certain we would be spared damage due to solid, state-of-the-art residential construction, the hurricane destroyed everything in its path.
3. He lost his professional job and was looking for a new career, so Darian moved to the tropics.
4. At midnight on a solitary road to nowhere, the accident occurred.
5. On its maiden voyage, the ship sank.

Answers 16.2: Answers will vary.

1. Owing to one great surfer, this beach will always be protected. (Depends on desired emphasis. Can also be: This beach will always be protected, owing to one great surfer.)
2. Out there in the boat that day, those two guys caught 52 crabs.
3. Causing great distress to all of these families and indeed the entire neighborhood, the fire took out 37 homes all along the ridge.
4. The best way for a lot of people to spend their vacations is probably in a hammock.
5. While the sacred words, "I am a Roman citizen," were on his lips, you ordered him to death.
6. Disrupting the vacations of thousands of travelers, without warning, the volcano erupted.
7. Unless this measure is clearly constitutional, I shall not vote for it.
8. When there was no danger, he feared, and when there was no sorrow, he wept.
9. Next to Washington, Greene was the ablest commander in the Revolutionary War.
10. The idea that animal consumption contributes to the world's largest problems forms the root for most veganism.

Answers 17.1: **Rewritten sentences will vary.**

1. <u>In his right hand was</u> the American flag, and <u>he held in his left</u> a tattered Spanish ensign.
   In his right hand was the American flag and *in his left* a tattered Spanish ensign.
2. <u>After having completed</u> the undertaking, and <u>when he had begun</u> another, he felt that his success was assured.
   After having completed the undertaking and *having begun* another, he felt that his success was assured.
3. Dinner was served in a spacious hall<u>, the panels of which</u> shone with wax, and <u>with the casings</u> hung with ivy.
   Dinner was served in a spacious hall*,* where *the panels* shone with wax and *the casings* hung with ivy.
4. <u>In one direction rolled</u> a train of wagons, and a company of soldiers <u>was marching in the other.</u>
   In one direction rolled a train of wagons, and *in the other marched* a company of soldiers.
5. <u>A large market place</u> *was* in the center, <u>with the council house</u> at the side.
   In the center was a *large market place*, and at the side was *the council house*.
6. <u>By day</u> Penelope wove the wondrous web; she unraveled her work <u>when it was dark</u>.
   By day Penelope wove the wondrous web; *by night* she unraveled her work.
7. The mob determined <u>to capture the king, imprison him</u>, and then, at the last, <u>they would try him</u> for his life.
   The mob determined *to capture the king, imprison him*, and then, at the last, *try him* for his life.
8. <u>Cooper wrote stories</u> of action and adventure; <u>the works of Hawthorne are weird</u> and strange.
   Cooper wrote action and adventure stories; *Hawthorne* wrote weird and strange ones.
9. <u>They were </u>of one generation, <u>and he had been brought up in</u> another.
   They were of one generation, and *he was of* another.
10. The first boy <u>accepted the generous offer</u>, but the second <u>thought it best not to agree.</u>
    The first boy *accepted the generous offer*, but the second boy *rejected it.*
11. He enjoyed <u>listening to others</u>, but others paid no attention <u>when he spoke</u>.
    He enjoyed *listening to others*, but others paid no attention *to him.*

***Example Answers 18.1*: Answers will vary.**

1. The damage to the car caused by the accident amounted to $1200.
2. Because of human behavior, many species are declining alarmingly.
3. Sea turtles, which return to their birthplace beaches to nest, won't come to bright beaches.
4. The man driving the car greeted me.
5. Traveling abroad with his brother has many advantages.
6. Working late, an American value, has infiltrated many industrialized societies.
7. The suicide rate among professionals, especially dentists, is alarming.
8. The banking industry, an industry only ostensibly there to help the people, profits from every war and every social downturn.
9. Judge Harrison ruled against the juvenile defendant, John's brother, sentencing him as an adult. *Or*
   Judge Harrison, John's brother, ruled against the juvenile defendant, sentencing him as an adult.
1. Writing sentences with appositives, such as these, isn't as easy as it looks.

***Example Answers 19.1*: Answers will vary.**

1. They took their coats when they realized it had snowed all night.
2. Little Red Riding Hood stared at her grandmother's teeth which had changed significantly since her last visit.
3. Brutus, who had been persuaded by Cassius, supported the assassination of Caesar.
4. At midnight, Cinderella's carriage turned back into a pumpkin. By lunch the next day, it had been cooked by the chef.
5. Our current leader cried because she had campaigned for months, but still lost the election.
6. She graduated from the university in five years instead of four because she had taken a year off to travel the world.
7. He couldn't buy his sister a present because he had spent all of his money before he remembered her birthday.

Answer 19.3: Answer will vary.

Notwithstanding the obscurity which thus envelops the date of the foundation of Vondervotteimittis, and the derivation of its name, there can be no doubt, as I said before, that it has always existed as we find it at this epoch. The oldest man in the borough can remember not the slightest difference in the appearance of any portion of it; and, indeed, the very suggestion of such a possibility is considered an insult. The site of the village is in a perfectly circular valley, about a quarter of a mile in circumference, and entirely surrounded by gentle hills, over whose summit the people have never yet ventured to pass. For this they assign the very good reason that they do not believe there is anything at all on the other side.

Answers 20.1: Answers will vary.
1. Then spake out brave Horatius.
2. We go off as the whip goes crack.
3. With her thousand voices, Earth praises God.
4. A beautiful thing is forever a joy.
5. On his raids, the rebel rides no more.
6. Wisdom is the principal thing; therefore, get wisdom.
7. Whatever he did, he did well.
8. If you are ashamed of your poverty and blush for your calling, you are a snob.
9. From the north blew a colder and louder gale wind.

Example Answers 21.13. Answers will vary.

1. (**Forcible**) The man outwitted the vicious dragon, bringing it to a violent death.
2. (**Vehement**) Looking crossways, running forward with sword raised high, yelling just before contact, the man reached the dragon and dug his sword far into the beast, slicing it square in the heart.
3. (**Elegant**) With raised sword glistening in the sunlight and an air of supreme confidence about him, showing courage and strength in full, the man came to the dragon and, deftly avoiding its deadly grasp, landed his sword square into the dragon's heart, pushing it in to the hilt, holding firmly until the dragon's movements ceased.
4. (**Brief**) The small man outsmarted the giant dragon, ending its life.
5. (**Precise**) Gathering his full strength, the man ran toward the dragon, landing his sword directly into the dragon's heart.
6. (**Copious**) Mounting the rock to enable him to square off with the dragon, the brave man drew his sword and, after a bit of a tussle, managed to land the tip of that sword squarely into the dragon's heart and, pushing through to the hilt, ended the dragon's miserable existence.
7. (**Diffuse**) In a display of pure bravery, or perhaps stupidity, as one might also perceive it, the man mounted the rock to allow him to reach the dragon's vulnerable chest and underbelly, and after a bit of a tussle with arms swinging wildly, he managed to hit his target squarely and sink that sword directly into the heart of the beast, bringing its miserable life to a quick and decided end.
8. (**Neat**) The weak little man, strong in character and brave in heart, shook vehemently as he sank his sword deep into the beast's heart.
9. (**Ornamental**) The man's demeanor was hardened with bravery and determination, his sword shining and hungry for a feast of its own as the man ran toward the fire-breathing beast, slicing its angry heart into two.
10. (**Feeble**) The man, not typically considered so brave or exceptional by those who knew him, that day found a core of determination and courage that brought him to the stone's apex, paralleling the dragon's heart, from where he took advantage of his position and newfound bravery to end the miserable dragon once and for all.
11. (**Loose**) Unencumbered by forethought or plan, disengaged from the wishes of others, the man, of his own accord, easily mounted the stone and, with a swift slash of his mighty sword, caught the vicious dragon in its heart, forever ending its threat to the people.
12. (**Plain**) The man was brave that day and killed the mighty dragon with one slash of his sleek sword.

REFERENCES

Albright, Evelyn May. *Descriptive Writing*. New York: Macmillan, 1911.

Baker, Franklin Thomas, and Ashley Horace Thorndike. *Everyday English: Book Two*. New York: Macmillan, 1913.

Blair, Hugh, and W. E. Dean. *Dr. Blair's Lectures on Rhetoric*. New York: Collins, Keese, 1836.

Craik, Henry. *Swift: Selections from His Works: Volume 2*. Oxford: Claredon, 1893.

Dalgleish, Walter Scott. *Introductory Text-book of English Composition*. Halifax, N.S.: A. & W. Mackinlay, 1886.

DeMille, James. *The Elements of Rhetoric*. New York: Harper & Bros., 1878.

Devlin, Joseph. *How to Speak and Write Correctlly*. New York: Christian Herald Bible House, 1910.

Emerson, Henry P., and Ida C. Bender. *Modern English*. New York: Macmillan, 1912.

English Grammar, Punctuation and Capitalization, Letter Writing. Scranton: International Textbook, 1905.

Espenshade, A. Howry. *The Essentials of Composition and Rhetoric*. Boston: D.C. Heath, 1904.

Gardiner, J. H., George Lyman Kittredge, and Sarah Louise Arnold. *Manual of Composition and Rhetoric*. Boston: Ginn, 1907.

Goldsbury, John. *A Sequel to the Common School Grammar*. Boston: J. Munroe, 1842.

Harvey, Thomas W. *Elementary Grammar and Composition*. Cincinnati: Van Antwerp, Bragg, 1880.

Huntington, Tuley Francis. *Elements of English Composition*. Toronto: Macmillan, 1915.

Lockwood, Sara Elizabeth Husted., and Mary Alice Emerson. *Composition and Rhetoric for Higher Schools*. Boston: Ginn, 1902.

Mooney, Margaret S. *Composition--Rhetoric from Literature: For High Schools, Academies and Normal Schools*. Albany, NY: Brandow Print., 1903.

Polk, Annie E. *Better Speech*. New York: Century, 1922.

Reed, Alonzo, and Brainerd Kellogg. *Graded Lessons in English*. New York: Maynard, Merrill, 1894.

Scott, Fred Newton, and Joseph Villiers Denney. *The New Composition-Rhetoric*. Boston: Allyn and Bacon, 1911.

Stebbins, Charles M. *A Progressive Course in English for Secondary Schools: Literature, Composition, Rhetoric, Grammar*. Boston: Sibley, 1915.

Stebbins, Charles M. *A Progressive Course in English: Literature, Composition*. Boston: Sibley, 1908.

Strunk, William, Jr. *The Elements of Style*. New York: Harcourt, Brace and Howe, 1920.

Swinton, William. *A Grammar Containing the Etymology and Syntax of the English Language*. New York: Harper & Bros., 1889.

Sykes, Frederick Henry. *English Composition for Grammar Schools*. New York: Charles Scribner's Sons, 1908.

The Greatest Works of the Greatest Authors. New York: H.W. Hagemann Pub., 1894.

Thomas, Joseph Morris, Frederick Alexander Manchester, and Frank William Scott.
Composition for College Students. New York: MacMillan, 1922.

Thorndike, Ashley Horace. *A Manual for Teachers: To Accompany the Elements of Rhetoric
and Composition.* New York: Century, 1905.

Thoreau, Henry David. *The Writings of Henry David Thoreau.* Boston: Houghton, Mifflin,
1898.

Webster, Noah. *A Manual of Useful Studies: For the Instruction of Young Persons of Both
Sexes, in Families and Schools.* Philadelphia: Jesper Harding, 1846.

Whately, Richard. *Elements of Rhetoric.* Oxford: Printed by W. Baxter for John Murray,
1830.

Williams, William. *Composition and Rhetoric: By Practice with Exercises, Adapted for Use in
High Schools and Colleges.* Boston: D.C. Heath, 1908.

Made in United States
North Haven, CT
14 December 2022

28852978R00117